**Coach Daryl's Colts**

(*Going For Two*)

Based off the remarkable true story that will

motivate, inspire, and capture your heart.

TO: Donna Seaman

Thanks for all that you do.

Please Review this amazing

true story.

Soins Fonto @smail.com   Coy MEDR

Www.50 Fon 2. net            #23

Printed in the United States of America

First Printing, 2018

ISBN 978-1-9858-3417-0

Library of Congress Cataloging- in- Publication Data
Coach Daryl's Colts / Corey McKinney, Author

# Table of Contents

# Dedication

## Making of a man

"This man was a man!  Not by birth but life. Not for his stature, but for his heart. Gold didn't seduce his hands, honor didn't turn his head. Dishonor didn't turn his feet: fear didn't curl his backbone, disappointment didn't crush his heart.

He was a man day and night, in the light and in the dark. In prosperity and in adversity. He had quality, and that - not pounds , nor inches, not color, - makes a man.

His grandeur was in his ideals, his beliefs, his practices and there the world should apply the gauges. For my hope of our society is to have more people like him.

-Because he was always there when you needed him.
-Because he always had a smile and a kind word
-Because he listen, cared, and understood
-Because he always could be counted upon to do what was best
-Because he always stood ready to help
-Because he was more than a coach
-Because we were proud to call him a father figure "

---Anonymous

This book is gratefully dedicated to
Coach Daryl Whittington

**Coach Daryl**

## With Gratitude

Thanks to my wife Octavia McKinney for listening to this story thousands of times over the years. Thanks to my two sons Erron and Jalen; my sister, Chundra; my mom, Cassandra McKinney for always being there; and my dad, Earl McKinney. Thanks to inspirational figures such as Steve Harvey, Rickey Smiley, Roc T., and my Pastor Dr. Al B Sutton Jr. Next I want to thank book writing coach Taurea Avant and my Radical Business Success Coach Doreen Rainey. Thanks to my book editor, Harriette Thompkins founder of Eagles Mount Editing. Also I would like to thank Aura Graphics for the book cover. Thanks to my family and all my friends who believed in my vision and dreams including Desmond Smoot, Lorenzo Ford, and Kelli Mims. Finally a special thanks to Mrs. Becky Whittington, Wilson, Amy, and Amanda for sharing Coach with us and opening up their home and hearts doing those years.

## Introduction

Going For Two

In today's society, there seems to be a lot of young men and women who lack the tools necessary to equip themselves for life. They are missing tools such as respect, self-pride, discipline, work ethic, and perseverance. All of these things can be taught and learned, but there has to be someone who takes the initiative to teach them. In life, there will be tons of ups and downs, disappointments, failures, accomplishments, happiness, sadness, good days, and challenging days. You will cross good people as well as bad ones. To sum it up, this life we live can be one long roller coaster ride. Living unequipped without these sustainable tools will leave a person struggling to cope with life. Some willing soul must take the initiative to teach the tools of life I mentioned earlier, or young people will look for substitutes that don't always lead to the best decisions. If these lessons are taught early on, young men and women will learn to depend on the right tools to make the right choices. A lot of people suffer in life because of not having anyone around to teach them life lessons. However, this doesn't have to be an excuse for you not to become successful. Parents are the first in line to educate their children on how to use these tools, but it just doesn't stop there. A variety of reasons has caused our youth not to have anyone to educate them on the tools of life. Many homes don't have fathers, some mothers are not present, some may have parents on drugs or just incapable of teaching the youth. There is a misconception that one person can't make a difference. That notion is so far from the truth. One person can make a difference in many lives, and for many generations to come. This person can be a parent, mother or father figure, teacher, coach, uncle, aunt, church member, or anyone who has the heart to help.  In this book, the difference maker comes in the form of a youth football coach by the name of Coach Daryl Whittington. Coach Daryl was a man who went over, and beyond the call of duty to impact the lives of kids forever. Coach was a teacher, a motivator, a disciplinarian, and most importantly a father figure. This book illustrates a coach that always went for two whether it was on the field or in our lives.

*Going For Two*

## Chapter 1
## The 65 lb: The Beginning

It was the summer of 1983 when a white male in his early 30s decided to allow his son to play youth football. This man was tall, wore a thick mustache, and had a very intimidating presence. This man who wore his blue jeans, cowboy boots and famous cowboy hat was known as Coach Daryl Whittington. Coach Daryl was married to his lovely wife, Mrs. Becky Whittington. The couple had three kids Amy, Amanda, and the youngest son Wilson. Coach and his family lived just minutes from downtown Birmingham Alabama, near Five Points South, an entertainment district on Birmingham's Southside. Their house was a nice three-story home one block over from Ramsey High, one of the city's magnet school. Coach also owned a machine shop located in Woodlawn off Georgia Road which is on the eastern side of Birmingham. His machine shop was approximately 20 minutes from his home. Coach worked hard, took pride in his work, and taking care of his family.

June 1983 Coach's son, Wilson, asked his dad to sign him up for the upcoming youth football season. Ironically, he wanted to play for the Crestwood Colts,from the American Youth Football League(AYFL). The Crestwood Colts played their games at Crestwood Park. The field was conveniently located 10 minutes from Coach Daryl's shop, so his dad decided to sign him up.

At the time, their were six teams including the 65 pound, 75 pound, 85 pound, 95 pound, 105 pound, and the 115 pound. The ages range from 5 to 14 years old. The 65-pound players had to be under seven years of age and at or below 65 pounds at the beginning of the season. The official weigh-in was mandatory to play on that pound for the year. If a player didn't make a particular weight, they had to go up to the next weight category. During the season, each player had to make the weigh-in weekly; if they didn't, the opposing coach could determine whether to allow the player to play or not. The park colors were green and white. Crestwood Park was equipped with a football field surrounded by a track, a playground located at the north end of the park; tennis courts at the south end, and it became our place of growth, learning, and competition. There were ten teams in the league. Some of the teams were from the inner city of Birmingham and others from the more rural areas of the city.

After tryouts and many drills, Wilson made the 65-pound team and was going to play quarterback. He was so excited to tell his dad. Coach Daryl was not going to coach his son, but on an afterthought, Coach Daryl decided to help out with the team. After lots of running and preparation, the team ended up with only 15 players. A combination of eight black kids and seven whites. Coach Daryl found it hard to watch a devastating season. There was nothing he could do being that he was only helping out. In 1983 the 65-pound Crestwood Colts began the season with a win. However, after the first game, they received the bitter taste of defeat for the rest of the season. In the final game of the year the 65-pound colts inked out a win; they finish the season with two wins and eight losses. Coach Daryl thought most of the losses were related to the boys not being taught things such as hard work, toughness, and discipline. Despite a disappointing season, Coach saw some potential with the boys, and there was a possibility that he could become the head coach. The first win might have been a little luck, but Coach Daryl saw the last victory as the beginning of a winning football team.

According to Coach Daryl's favorite football coach, Paul "Bear" Bryant, building a winning football team is something that cannot be accomplished overnight. The Crestwood Colts' 65-pound team had developed an infamous reputation as easy conquerors among the other teams in the AYFL; therefore, each team in the league looked forward to playing the Colts.

My My My; what a difference one year can make. At the end of the season, the head coach from the 65-pound team decided not to return for the following season. After a long talk with his family, Coach Daryl agreed to take the challenge and become the head coach for the Crestwood Colts for the upcoming season. Coach thought the lack of wins was a direct correlation between undisciplined boys and soft coaching. Coach knew what the boys needed: a hardcore method of a disciplinarian approach to football. To begin, Coach Daryl had to face the difficult problem of rebuilding a team. With the previous head coach leaving, seven of the fifteen players also were not coming back. With only eight players remaining, Coach knew he had to go out and get some players and coaches to make up a team. The remaining players were Wilson, Coach's son, Chester McGlocton, Jesse Hubbard, Devarus Patterson (sparkplug), Jeremy Mosely, Mickal Thomas, Preston Pratt, and T J Slaughter. These were the only returning players along with the returning defense coach, Coach Pratt. Mrs. Dot (Rip), the mom of Mickal Thomas, knew a former, tough Woodlawn High School football player and recommended him as a good fit to coach the Colts--Tim Cowan. Coach Tim, relatively light-skinned, muscular, and built like a tank, carried a hard nose demeanor. Coach Tim would serve as the offensive coordinator and work with the running backs. Tim recommended one of his high school teammates, James Love, to come aboard.

Love played linebacker at Woodlawn high School and was projected as a fierce competitor, and seemed intimidating. His sternness demanded any players attention. Lastly, Coach Carmichael was picked up to help the offensive line. So here was the line up: Coach Daryl Whittington, head coach; Coach Tim and Coach Carmichael, offensive coaches; and Coach Love and Coach Pratt, defensive coaches. Now that the staff was in place, there was still only eight players returning.

So now it's the summer of 1984, and Coach Daryl and his staff had to recruit some players to try out for the team. Despite the slim pickings, Coach Daryl still decided to hold tryouts. Anyone would have thought he would have taken whoever showed up to the field. Not with Coach Daryl-- he went through with the tryouts; he knew what he needed to build a quality team. Coach Daryl's tenacity led him to some of the roughest inner-city neighborhoods to pass out flyers for the tryouts. These communities were predominantly black, heavily drug infested, filled with gangs, violence, and fighting. All of them were notorious areas in Alabama and maybe the entire South. Let us keep in mind that the year is 1984 which was only twenty years removed from the harsh Civil Rights era in Birmingham, AL. One of the neighborhoods mentioned above, Kingston Projects, is where I grew up. Kingston is located only a few miles from the Birmingham Airport. The area was infamous for its gang violence and drug dealing. Living conditions were overcrowded, and shootings and death were almost a commonplace. Despite drug dealing and gang violence being present, there were plenty of friendly people with a lot of neighborhood pride mixed in as well. Along with that neighborhood pride, there was a unique closeness. We took care of our own. If you were from Kingston, you were like family.

Some of us from the neighborhood are still close now. Avondale Projects, Southtown Projects, High Chapparal (the Shep), and Gate City were all places that Coach Daryl bravely went to recruit. These areas were similar in demographics and makeup to Kingston projects. Along with these areas, players came from a variety of places located throughout Birmingham, Alabama.

One day, one of the flyers reached me in Kingston. This where I received my invite for, what I didn't know then, one of the biggest tryouts of my life. I was reared in a sports-oriented family: Uncles Ervin, BB, and Barry Sullivan played sports; Uncle Robert, Uncle Theotis (mule), and my Dad played and coached sports; my cousins Derek and Robert Slater III also played football at Hayes High School. There was no doubt that signing up was in my bloodline. Meanwhile, back at my elementary school, the Kingston Cougars, word was spreading about the tryouts. Over at Avondale elementary, Terrail Saffo was spreading the word to a few more guys such as ;Cameron Mitchell, Juan Saffo (To-Jo) Saffo, Reginald Wright, and James Calhoun. There were a lot of local students who were already playing in a different youth football league called Metro. The Metro League, filled with kids from the inner city, was considered to be the toughest of them all. Teams such as East Lake Cowboys, Ensley Broncos, A.G Gaston (Bham and Bessemer ), and West End. So the word was all over Birmingham about the Crestwood tryouts starting in July, 1984.

I'll never forget the first day of tryouts. I guess word of mouth travels because we had over sixty boys who came out. It was a very hot and humid day around 90°. This turnout was overwhelming and unexpected, considering that the prior year left the team with only eight players. Coach Daryl wore his famous cowboy hat, t-shirt, and cowboy boots. Alongside Coach were his assistants Love, Pratt, Carmichael, and Tim. For the coaches to pinpoint who was in shape and to identify players for skill positions, the practices consisted of tons of running and agility drills. All of the coaches were intense, and there was a whole lot of yelling and cursing. So of course some players didn't come back for day two. Some of the parents didn't like the language and hard nature, so they didn't bring their child back. Some players found the tone a bit shocking and surprising but all of us from the hood was used to it. Honestly, I guess you can say, to us it just felt like being at home. These practices were conducted like a Division I or pro-style camp. We were pulled and tucked all kinds of ways. In the running drills, guys had the opportunity to throw, catch, and run routes. You can almost tell which guys were going to be the lineman and which of the guys would possibly be skill players. Amongst the crowd, a couple of guys stood out throwing the ball, including Wilson. His accuracy was on point, and James Calhoun's arm strength was incredible. James could probably throw the ball 30-40 yards already. Most of the players were either seven or eight years of age, and we did have a few players that were six; we had one player who was five named Davaus Patterson (sparkplug). Five-year-old Plug was forced to play up with us because of his weight. The offensive coaches ran drills on how to carry the ball, how to stay low while blocking, and route running. Defensive coaches employed dummies to show us the proper way to tackle. We were taught how to attack each hole depending on where the play was going. Also how to back pedal and turn your hips defending pass plays. These agility drills and running went on for the next several weeks. Of course, more and more players fell off and faded away, as it seemed the practices became harder and harder. One on one drills running routes and defending were intense. Nobody wanted to have a bomb caught on them. The one on one blocking drills and trying to get to the q/b were fierce. All of these things went on throughout July until the big day in August. I have one word: PADS. I can remember just like it was yesterday; that Friday after practice everyone was fitted for helmets and shoulder pads. We knew that the following Monday was going to be a whole different story. The entire park, filled with excitement, they knew that everyone in the league would be in pads on Monday. All six teams shared the field during practice; we were the second smallest team on the field, and we were also thrilled to see the big boys hit as well.

The upkeep of the park was something to be proud of; the home side had green bleachers and steps. The concession stand was next to the bleachers. On the backside of the concessions was the equipment room, and it had steps that led up to the booth where we heard the announcers describe play by play. In the equipment room, all the players came week after week before each game to weigh in to see if they were eligible to play. The playground described earlier would be heavily utilized by players after the game on Saturdays. The visitors used the opposite side of the park parallel to Crestwood Blvd. This street led to a once busy mall called Century Plaza. Lots of people would stop by and watch the games when leaving the mall.

So the first Monday of August hit and we are all in full pads. You can feel the intensity in the air. The coaches were fired up and ready to go. By this time the 65 players have decreased to around fifty. Not bad, and it was the most of any one team in the park. A vast difference was made plain in the guys that played the prior year versus the ones like myself of whose it was their first time out. Before Coach Daryl would allow anyone to make contact with another player, we ran drills over and over again on the proper way to block, and tackle using the dummies. Drills for blocking taught us how to use the three-point stance properly and we learned that dropping your bottom and keeping your head up was important. Next, we were taught that having balance and not putting all of your weight behind you is crucial, too. Coach used bars that you had to stay under when firing off the ball. We were taught to stay low and drive the dummy until you heard the echo of the whistle. When blocking, we were shown first how to get your splits from the person next to you. Getting splits from the person next to you means that you make sure you are one foot away from the person next to you, to prevent tripping each other. Then we were shown how to get your head and shoulders on the correct side of the dummy to direct the defensive player away from where the play is going. We practiced cross blocks and trap blocks all using the dummies. On top of all of this, we ran drills on how to block moving targets in the open field. Mainly this was to teach guys not to clip or block a player in the back. Potential offensive lineman ran drills on how to pass protect by using their hands and feet, and potential receivers ran routes and used the dummies held by coaches to make their cuts. Coaches employed the dummies to jam us at the line of scrimmage where we had to use our hands to get free. Coach and his staff taught these unforgettable lessons in football.

On the defensive side, Coach Love and Pratt taught us the fundamentals of how to make a tackle. I see players today on all levels, especially the youth level that are trying to make tackles incorrectly. We learned how to tackle using our shoulder pads and legs. Next, you would need to keep your eyes on the offensive player's waist. Then we had to make sure that you kept your head up to avoid neck and back injuries. After all of this we were all set on how to tackle. Eyes on the waist, head up, lead with your shoulder pads, wrap up, then drive with your legs. How to tackle is something that stuck with me for the next six years.

All positions were open with the 50 players even with the eight who returned. Running was our life and seemed that we would never stop running. Just when we thought the hitting would start, (we all looked forward to hitting), Coach had another agenda. To be the team he had envisioned for us, we needed everyone to be in better shape. So on the first week of pads, we watched all of the other pounds 65, 85, 95, 105 and the 115 hitting, yelling and playing football. Meanwhile, we were running like Carl Lewis and the 1984 Olympic track team. Man, I tell you, I thought, there was no way that any other team could stand this type of conditioning. The humid heat in the South was burning on us like no tomorrow. While the other pounds were hitting, we were learning footwork, working with your hands, blocking techniques, tackling techniques, tip drills, and angles to the ball on offense and defense. We couldn't help but to glance around at our peers from time to time. Unsurprisingly, after all of the daily drills, the running, the yelling and cursing by the coaches, we ended the week with about thirty-five players remaining. Some guys just couldn't keep up: only the strong survived. A few parents removed players and cursed Coach, saying things like this is not a camp for college kids. Nevertheless, the practices continued with no changes. The next week the coaches met and started to separate players on offense and defense. Players such as ToJo stood out in the hitting drills and T J in the blocking drills.

 The practices usually started with stretching which at the end which Tim and Love killing us with those dreaded six inches. The dreaded six inches is where you lie on your back and hold both legs up off the ground six inches. Man, it seemed like we had to hold our legs up forever. Any player who dropped their legs before time just added more time. I can still hear Tim saying, "up, open, close, down." And on the last one-- "open, close, open, close, open, close--hold it, hold it." By the time he said, "drop 'em," I think we had dropped everything we had in us. So after the stretching, we always had to run two laps around the field. I would always be in the front showing hustle, but also I knew that the faster I completed the run, the more time I'll have to rest and wait for everyone to finish. After the two laps, we were broken up into groups depending on your size and speed. Some of the possible offensive linemen went to Carmichael. The potential quarterbacks as running backs and receivers went with Daryl and Tim. Everyone else went with Love and Pratt on defense. First, we worked on plenty of one on one hitting drills: That's when two guys are lying on their backs and getting up to run and tackle. Watching this, made you know who would be good tacklers. Players like To-Jo, Reginald, Dewayne, and Quincy were all good hitters. Guys who could run the ball, like Andy, Mike, and Cam, stood out in the crowd. We ran three on two drills where two guys blocked, and one ran the ball against two defenders, our coaches wanted to see who could fight off the blocks and still tackle. This type of drill typically favored the offense. We also ran one on one drills, with four dummies spread out three feet apart, the runner had the option to run between any of the three holes between the dummies; with the defender trying to tackle.  Everyone knew that if you didn't pick the first two options, you had no choice but to take the last opportunity. This was one of our favorite drills.  By then the defender knew where you were going and would be waiting for you. The coaches made sure that in each exercise every person made contact mimicking how it was taught with the practice dummies.  If anyone ran away from contact or used the wrong mechanics, the practice would stop, and that person would go one on one until they got it right or was not scared anymore.  If you did not win the battle, trust me, fear was not going to be the reason why.  Everything's was about competition, hard work, and hustle. Between every drill, we transitioned to the next phase of practice by running.  Absolutely no walking around was allowed. These hard conditions and tough coaches, once again, caused more and more kids to drop off.  After the first week in pads, we were down to around thirty players. Looking back, you knew that Coach was looking for mental toughness and discipline.  Some kids were so undisciplined that they weren't going to ever fit in on this team. So now it's mid-August and a few more players fell off.  Our practices were like boot camp or basic training for the Army. The in your face hardcore style of coaching we were getting was just too much for a few. Growing up in Kingston, the profanity was a part of everyday culture, so it didn't bother us.  What was important to us is that the coaches taught us and knew what was best for us. Ironically, the players that decided to quit left a formulating team.  Everyone received their fair trial and although some guys tried out for positions, knowing they couldn't  play, but Coach gave them a shot anyway. Ultimately guys like Terrail and Tojo separated out as receivers.  Wilson and James headed the quarterback position. Andy became a dominating fullback.  Mike led the war at tailback and Cam, at wingback. Probably the meanest players and the fiercest group were the offensive linemen. Remind you that at this age group running the ball would happen most of the time. Coach knew that a sturdy offensive line would be vital. Players such as Reg James, T J, Demetrius, and Mauricus filled those slots. Coach Tim who was a former offensive stud would always walk around yelling to us, "Four yards a pop, four yards a pop," while the offense was running the ball. He said, "If you don't get four yards, it's a win for the defense."

The defense had begun to form. Players such as Jeremy, small, but quick, snagged the noseguard position; Jesse and Munt, defensive tackles. Dwayne and Quincy played inside linebackers. Randy and Charles played corner; Charlie and Preston worked at safety. As for me, I played defensive end. Coach Love ran a 5-2 base defense. We also ran plenty of different schemes from that base that we practice over and over daily. Another defense we ran was a 5-3 or sometimes 5-5 stack. The 5-5 is when we stacked the linebackers directly behind the noseguard and two defensive tackles. We used the strong safety as one of the linebackers. Coach Love ran a lot of stunts out of these sets. Sometimes the middle linebacker would give the signal by tapping the noseman on the left or right bottom to indicate to him which way to go. Depending on the alignment, he would send a defensive lineman one way and the linebacker the opposite direction. Making this move would usually give the offensive lineman lots of problems. We were taught leverage and how to block inside out. No matter what the defense showed, always block inside out. Coach showed us how to cross-block which would be pivotal to our run game success. A cross-block is when our offensive end would block down on the defensive tackle, and the offensive tackle would pull out and block out the defensive end. We also learned how to trap block: when you did not block the defensive lineman on purpose to make him think he is free and another lineman comes along from the opposite side to take him out. We all learned multiple positions, so I got plenty of knowledge playing wide receiver on the second team.

Coach Daryl, a self-taught coach, read plenty of books and followed the legend, Paul Bear Bryant. Coach's philosophy stood as your team is only as good as your last man. That's the reason everyone had to compete. Too often coaches in our time focus only on the starters or the best players, but on our team, players one through twenty-five received the same teaching. When there were mistakes, the one through twenty-five received the same chewing out. Some came in the form of getting yelled at, cursed out, kicked in the rear-end with those cowboy boots, snatched by the facemask or just plain old snatched up. None of it was ever to harm us, we knew he wanted to make us better and to become champions. Next coach went out and purchased some green, red, and blue practice jerseys. Before I get into what they were for, let me now stop and thank Mrs. Becky Whittington for washing and bringing these jerseys to practice every day. Moms, can you imagine today going to work, taking care of your family and washing practice jerseys daily and game jerseys for a large team on Saturdays. Thank you from the boys, Mrs. Becky. So once all of the players were in position, we found out about the jerseys. The offense would be wearing blue at practice. The defense would be wearing red. However, we didn't understand what would happen with the green jerseys. Let's be clear, everything we did was about competition. Typically on Monday's, we put out offensive gameplay for that upcoming Saturday. Our defense would show the defensive scheme of our opponent. Tuesdays, the defensive game plan was installed. Our offense would run and show the opponent offensive look. Wednesdays we would work on short yardage, two-point conversions, and red zone offense and defense. Thursdays were special teams. However, every day our finale was the offense against the defensive scrimmage. These scrimmages were knockout, drag-out battles. If you ask a defensive player today who won the overall battles, he would say the defense; and the same goes for an offensive player. The battles were about scoring and stopping the offense from scoring. Six teams were sharing the field, simultaneously, so we may have had the 30-yard line to the end zone by the end of the day. Each time the offense scored, that was a point for them; and if we stopped them, that was a point for us. Coach would always use a odd number for the weekly battles. So by the end of Thursday practice, there would be a winner of the scrimmages; hence the green jerseys. The weekly number was always a number like seventeen, twenty-one or twenty-five. Any number that someone can win. Coach would announce the winner, and most times, going into Thursday we knew who had the lead or if it was tied. If the defense found out we were up 14-11 for the week, we had a little breathing room. Both sides wanted to win every single drive, so generally, the score would always close on Thursday. After the Thursday scrimmage, Coach would announce the winner and that side of the ball won the right to wear the green jerseys at practice that Friday. The Friday practices would be wearing helmets and shorts or sweatpants, only. Ah man, you had bragging rights for a whole week. Not only could you brag, but there you had the pleasure of other perks, as well. Remember after stretching we had to run two laps daily? Well, the green jerseys only had to run one. (competition again). Coach faithfully brought water to practice for us to stay hydrated. On Fridays there were two coolers. One with water and the other with Gatorade for the green jerseys. I don't know about you, but Gatorade tastes like heaven when you're outside sweating and busting your tail for two hours in the hot sun. The first water break was right after the two laps, so if you were a green jersey, you were already sipping on Gatorade, while the losers are having to run another lap and then come back to get their ice, cold water. What a good feeling it was to win. Nobody wanted that extra lap and water. A little trash talking would go on at this point. And the final perk of having the green jerseys was that you received fewer wind sprints on Fridays. Every practice ended with wind sprints by the entire team. Now if all of that is not enough to get you motivated to compete then I don't know what will get you going. In our Friday practices, we had fun with competitive wind sprints. Coach would place our fastest two players, Cam and Randy, on opposite teams. Coach would then match every player by speed, as even as possible, and distribute them to each player. The slowest player who was 5-year-old Plug. Each week, Coach alternated Plug in between teams, to make things seemly fair. Sparkplug use to give his all in the races. It was a treat to see what strategy the team would choose when Sparkplug was with them. Sometimes the team would ask Plug to run first and try to make up the stagger. Some would prefer to create a lead and let Plug bring it home last. Reflecting, I don't know if any of it worked, but sparkplug use to be hustling to try and make his team win. The race would start with both teams in the end zone in a single file line, separated by about ten yards. Each player had to run to the 25-yard-line turnaround and run back and tag a teammate. Once the last player runs that would end the race. The coaches would stand on the 25 to make sure everyone followed the rules. I think the coaches may have let Plug turn around at the 22 if they were loosing (hilarious). A fun way to end Friday practice and another strategy that Coach implemented for an opportunity for competition in our practices. After enduring a grueling hot summer, the players and Coach Daryl headed into his first year as head coach for the upcoming 75 lb Colts football season.

CRESTWOOD
1983
65 lb. TEAM

## Chapter 2
## The 75 lb: Getting Ready To Roll

Coach Daryl is in for the long haul. The season fired off
with a load of intensity, rising higher and higher as we were
moving closer to our first game. I'm quite sure that all of
our opponents could not wait to play us. The team we
would have to face first was Center Point. As luck would
have it, we would play the AYFL (American Youth Football
League) runner-up from the previous year. They were a
two-loss team that played in the championship game as
the 65-pound team in 1983. They were talented and well
coached as a unit. Mike and Andy fathers, Charles Sr. and
Lewis, recorded videos of our opponents and gave them to
Coach for us to watch film and scout.  It just so happened
that Lewis had the game film from the previous year of
Center Point verses the Colts. The Colts lost  pretty bad,
but Coach discovered that they frequently executed
against us an onside kick during their kickoffs. With that
knowledge, Coach taught us at our last Thursday practice
to plan for it over and over again. For anything that came
our way, we would remain prepared. Coach Daryl and Tim
started to put the offensive game plan together.
Carmichael worked to put his line in check:  Tackles,
Demetrius and Reg; guards, T. J.  and Mauricus; and
center, James.  A catalyst, this offensive line was
responsible for most of our success, considering that at
this age the most you are expected to do is run the ball.
These guys were mean, tough, and would block you 20
yards down the field. They used cross blocks and trap
blocks to perfection. Terrail and ToJo were hardnose
blockers with speed and could catch very well. Andy Rice,
the fullback for our team, reminded you of a modern day,

Derrick Henry, when he played for Alabama; with the size, but with more speed. Andy was the biggest, fastest, powerful runner coming into the league. He could run right over you and had the ability to make defenders miss. A little scary. Andy, by no means, shied away from contact. Mike Thomas was named the starting tailback. Mike, a hard nose, short, stocky runner with huge powerful legs, ran extremely hard and it was difficult for one man to bring down. The wingback, Cameron Mitchell, Cam, was one of the fastest player, if not the fastest on the team. Cam, reminded you of the USC days of Reggie Bush. Cam, smooth, super quick, and a catcher, ranked as a physical runner, too. Finally, on offense, Coach Daryl's son, Wilson "Willie" Whittington. Wilson was tall, smart and an accurate thrower. You had to be sharp to play quarterback on our team because even on the 75lb team, Coach made the quarterback come half way to the sideline to receive the play. Coach would hand signal to call every play to the quarterback from his famous play chart. Once Coach Daryl hand signaled the play, then the quarterback would relay the message in the huddle to the team, run to the line, and execute the play. Immediately after the play, the quarterback had to look over to the sideline to get the information for the next play and meet everyone in the huddle, once again. It was practiced over and over again until it became second nature. Coach's play chart had short yardage plays, goal line plays, long yardage plays, and two-point conversions also. I was lucky enough to obtain a part of the famous playbook which contained the following plays:

(Short yardage)
1.Proset wing right strong cross-block 46
2. Proset wing right strong cross-block 16
3. Proset wing right slam bam 42
4. Proset wing left slam bam 21
5. Proset wing right strong 21 draw

(End Sweeps)
1.Proset wing right weak quick toss 28
2. Wing right weak 18 sweep
3. Wing right weak 37 reverse
4. Wing right weak fake reverse
5. Wing right weak student body 37
6 Wing right strong red dog 37

(Pass Plays)
1.Wing right strong rollout pass 81
2. Wing right strong quick slant pass 87
3. Wing right strong drop back pass 28
(Reverses)
1.Double Wing Double reverse 28
2. Double Wing Fake Double Reverse Keeper.

Unfortunately, this is only a small portion of the playbook, but a great treasure. If a teammate played offense, they had to learn all of the plays. If you were the quarterback, you had to read and know the signals from the sideline. Oh yes, we went over the plays hundreds of times. James also held the position of quarterback. They would trade out spots: Wilson played center when James went to quarterback, and vice versa. James, a big guy, had a cannon for an arm. Other notable guys were Randy Albright, who arguably between him and Cam, was the fastest on the team. Randy was fast as lightning, if he ever got outside, you could call it quits. The team's second-string fullback was T. J.  All of the second team players received just as many reps as the first team, so if anyone went down, the team didn't miss a beat.  More notable guys like Jesse and Munt played well a defensive tackles; Jeremy and Sparkplug at nosemen; and To-Jo, Dewayne, and Quincy were wreaking havoc at inside backers.  A few guys played on both sides:  Mike, Andy, and Cam.  Coach Love and Pratt installed several defenses, including our favorite called Red Dogg: when everyone except the two safeties blitzed.  Redd Dogg turned out disastrous for every opponent we played.

In those last couple of days of practice, we must have gone over every situation you could have thought of. After practice, the Friday before the first game, Coach passed out our green t-shirts and shorts. The tops were green in color with Crestwood wrote on the front in white and our number on the back also in white. We wore these under our pads for the game and during weigh in on Saturdays. Coach Daryl and his wife Mrs. Becky purchased these for us to wear.  Weigh-ins were crucial.  After practice, if you weighed over the 75 lbs, you would have to run laps to try to get the weight down by the next day. If anyone was close to not making the weight the next day, they had to run more laps. Some were given laxatives to help; others had to come to the park early the next morning and run with garbage bags on trying  to drop a few pounds or ounces. So Saturday morning finally arrived, and our first game is at our park. Since we are the second smallest team that meant our game would be at 10:30 am, due to the sixty-five-pound team playing at 9 am. Coach Daryl would make it to the field around 8 am and line the field up for the first game. We had to be at the park at 9 am in our green t-shirts and shorts. We came to watch and support our sixty-five-pound team. Coach taught us that at Crestwood we were all family, he made sure our fellow Colts had our cheers. At halftime of the sixty-five-pound game, we had to weigh in. Munt and James barely made the weigh-in and had to do a little extra running that morning and not eat anything. Their parents had food waiting for them after they made the weight. Right before the game, James' mom would be watchfully waiting at the entrance of the field with his burger and drink. After the weigh-ins, we would load up on the famous green bus: The legendary Big Green Machine. So as we're getting on our pads, Coach would always come on the bus to give us the pre-game speech. Most of the time he had to stop us from playing around and acting up (To-Jo, Quincy, Reg) lol. Coach Love and Tim would come on the bus firing us up with chants like:

*We want some meat!*
*Gotta have that meat!*

*What we gone do? (Coach)*
*Do it to 'em! (us)*
*What we gone do? (Coach)*
 *Do it to 'em! (us)*
*Strike that match! (Coach)*
*Fire it up! (us)*
*What we gone do! (Coach)*
*Do it to 'em! (us)*

After getting fired up, we would unload off the bus and head down the ramp in numerical order. As we walked toward the field, we continued our ritual of chants:

*Colts get ready to roll,*
*Colts get ready to roll! (clap-clap-clap)*

*Colts get ready to roll,*
*Colts get ready to roll! (clap-clap*
*-clap)*

Man, I'm getting goosebumps just thinking about it. We were so fired up on the way to the field. I think we intimidated some teams before the game even started. Our parents, especially the dedicated Moms Squad, would beat us to the field and stood with the cheerleaders outside the gate as we entered the field. I want to give special thanks to the Dad's that were at all of the games: Charles Rice Sr, Lewis Thomas, Mr. Albright, Mr. Mosley, and others. However, this Moms Squad was off the chain. They were some unbelievable, faithful, ride or die soldiers. They were at every game we played, home or away. The Moms Squad would be cheering, running up and down the field, and chanting with the cheerleaders and players. They had every cheer and dance down to perfection. They met us after every game singing, "We are proud of you, and we are proud of you." (clap-clap-clap). They faithfully attended every game; whether it was in the 90-degree weather, the rain, cold, or snow. Nothing, and I mean nothing stopped them from supporting us. Moms such as the late Barbara Hubbard, who would always assist with the cheerleaders. Others like Diane Mosely, Bernice Albright, Ms Provitt, Ms Saffo, Marilyn Mitchell, Mrs. Slaughter, Laura Calhoun, and Cassandra McKinney just to name a few. The leaders of the Mom Squad were our wonderful team moms Becky Whittington, Dot Thomas, and Jackie Rice.

We entered the game as heavy underdogs. Nobody expected us to win against Center Point. We always warmed up in the south end zone. After stretching and warming up, we all lined up in numerical order between the goal post. With our helmets off, we were called one by one in order by our announcer. As our names were called, we would run to the 50-yard-line and turn left to go toward our sideline. We were, no doubt, decked in the best gear: uniforms white with Crestwood wrote in green across the chest, socks that were solid green at the top and white halfway down the bottom (Coach purchased these) and green wristbands and green hand towels to match. I can still here our announcer call us on to the field:

*Here are the Crestwood Colts seventy-five-pound team coached by Coach Daryl Whittington: #10 Charlie Glenn, #12 Dewayne Tolbert, #14 Willie Whittington, #22 Cameron Mitchell, #23 Corey McKinney, #24 T.J. Slaughter, #26 Preston Pratt, #32 Randy Allbright, #33 Mikal Thomas, #34 Jeremy Mosley, #42 Charles Stephens, #44 James Calhoun , #45 Andy Rice, #54 Edmund Provitt, #55 Matt #56 Chester Mcglocton, #63 Jesse Hubbard, #68 Darius, #70 Reginald Wright, #74 Demetrius Burks, #83 Mauricus Green, #86 Juan (To-Jo)Saffo, #88 Terrail Saffo, #98 Quincy Weaver, and last but not least #99 Devarus (Sparkpug) Patterson.*

These were the survivors that made it starting from the over 60 players who tried out.

Center Point won the toss-up and tried their anticipated onside kick right from the beginning. What they did not know was that we had practice for that, now, for a couple of weeks. They shifted to the left, and we shifted to the left. Right off, at the first play, I knew that our team was a different one from the team on last year. We dominated on both lines of scrimmage from the beginning. We stopped them on their first drive and forced them to punt. On this pound there was no actual punt, so the referees just walked the ball 40 yards out. Mike (#33) capped off our first drive with a 20-yard touchdown run. Our defense was stellar; we shut them out of the end zone the entire game with no points. Reg, Dewayne, and Munt led the way with outstanding play. Our offensive line was dominant all game which led two more touchdown runs. One from Andy and one from Cam. We ended the game with an 18-0 victory.

What a difference one year can make. After the game, we left the field headed toward our sideline and guess who was there to celebrate us? Yep, you guessed it! The Moms Squad singing, "We are proud of you, and we are proud of you," We were chanting,

*We stomped those bulldogs down to the ground!*
*Hey, Hey!*
*We told you yesterday that we were gonna clown!*

Coach congratulated us on our first win, but also informed that there was still room for a lot of improvement. This win against Center Point was Coach Daryl's first win, as head coach, and our first win as a team. The question loomed over our heads, could this be the start of something special, or is this a repeat from last year where the sixty-five-pound team won its first game? Only, time would tell, but I believe deep in our hearts, we knew that this was special.

Celebrations had come to a halt, as we were back on the practice field the following Monday. The coaches were all over us. You would have thought that we had lost 18-0, the way they were on us. The practice was intense, and the competition was at its highest.

We had our first road game coming, and the coaches wanted to make sure we would be focused on playing away without the home field crowd. Repetition was crucial to everything we did. Every single play ran over and over until the execution was perfect. It is important to note that we were getting our calls for the plays from our coaches on the sidelines with hand signals. The offense and the defensive calls were done this way, but not by accident. When we scrimmaged at practice, things were ran this way. If anyone missed an assignment or made an error, it was hell to pay. You better watch out for Coaches cowboy boot print on your butt pad, or a slap across the helmet or maybe a good old fashion cursing out. If a player missed a block, tackle or acted like they were scared, the practice would stop immediately. Whenever a player displayed fear or someone or ran away from a player, Coach would make them go one on one with that player. You would continue to battle until that fear was gone. You may not ever have won the individual battle, but the fear of that player would be gone. Psychologically, we were taught that no one was going to have a fear of anyone and that no one would know that you were afraid of them. Show no fear. You can't allow any player to know you are afraid of them because they will continue to pick on you. A form of self-respect, adopting this mentality, caused us all not to be afraid of any team we played, regardless of their size. Discipline and repetition were critical, and the second and third string players were treated no differently, and were just as involved in practice, as the first string players.

We ran this hitting drill a couple of times at practice called the Bull Ring. The drill worked on your footwork, quickness, and toughness. The selected player would stand in the middle of a circle chopping his feet turning in a circle. The surrounding players would come and hit the player chosen in the center, on the coach's command. The inside player would not know which player was coming. You had to keep your head on a swivel. As soon as you hit one player, another one was coming for you from the opposite side. We had run this drill a couple of times before, but at this particular practice, we had a problem. At this practice, our offensive guard, Maurcius, was inside the ring doing well. He had just squared off with a player when coach pointed out Andy to come and hit him from the opposite side. Andy was a big, fast runner, and a great hitter. Mauricus finished his hit and tried to turn to his right to take on Andy. He didn't quite get fully squared up and dipped his shoulder down to hit the charging Andy; however, the impact was too much for a side hit. Mauricus ended up breaking his collarbone and would be out for weeks. That was the last time Coach Daryl allowed us to run that drill. Coach never intended for anyone to get hurt by it.

In spite of this tragedy, we finished the week of practice and battled for the green jerseys as we prepared for our next opponent, Pinson. Coach Daryl noticed that there had been some players coming to practice late. Many of us didn't have rides to practice, and we had to walk with our shoulder pads and helmets every day. The kids from the inner city projects such as Avondale, Kingston, Gate City, and High Chaparral walked daily. Coming from Kingston, it was an approximately a 50-minute walk for us, and a distance of around five to six miles to get to the park. The walk seemed even longer walking over a few hills carrying your equipment in the scalding heat. Being late for practice always carried a cost of running extra laps. Once coach found this out, he decided to *Go For Two* and help us out by creating a route in which he would pick us up for practice and take us home on his bus, The Green Machine. We sometimes made jokes saying to Coach if we were late getting to practice, now, he had to run the extra laps. Keep in mind that this is 1984 and only 20 years removed from the harsh civil rights era in Birmingham, AL. Now here is Coach Daryl a white man coming into some of the most dangerous areas in the city for his boys. Not only was our team picked up but provided there was room, other Crestwood players in the same neighborhoods could ride as well. The players on the larger pound teams found out quick not to play around with Coach. I remember we were in the middle of Gate City Projects and one of the players from another pound was mouthing off at Coach. Immediately, Coach stopped the bus in the middle of the street and went to the back of the bus, and gave that player a good old fashion cursing out. You could have heard a pin drop the rest of the ride to practice. They found out that Coach was a strict disciplinarian and didn't play games.

I can remember rolling through Kingston, and some gangsters tried to shake coach up, but he never backed down. They were saying things like get out of our neighborhood, and all of them were strapped (loaded with guns). These gangsters had no problem with shooting someone and taking their life. As they approached the bus, Coach's right hand was easing down under his seat. What they didn't know was that coach kept his 38 pistol under the seat as well. I knew the guys; however, this was my coach, I thought, and for a couple of seconds I felt that this could turn into a dangerous situation. All I could do is pray nothing went wrong. Coach would respond to them by saying I'm just here for my boys fellas. It didn't take long, especially since all of the gangsters knew us, and saw what coach was doing for us to like him. They ended up gaining crazy respect for him. They even started to protect him. One of the leaders and one of the most hardened gangsters in the neighborhood told coach one day before practice, "I like what you are doing with our boys, and if you ever have any problems from anyone, Coach D., you just let me know. " Coach Daryl just smiled and said, "ok." Another one of the gang members asked Coach, "What time is the game this Saturday. I heard y'all won last week." Coach responded, "10:30 am, M. J." Coach knew the guys by name. M. J. said to Coach, "I can't get up that early, I am just getting in the bed about four or five in the morning after being on the block all Friday night." We all laughed, but Coach invited them anyway. Surprisingly enough, these guys started coming to the games and supporting us on Saturdays.

So next we rolled around to Saturday morning, and after picking us up, we all head to the park to prepare for our first road game. Coached checked all of the player's weight to make sure no one was over 75 lb. We had on our green t-shirts and shorts as we packed into the Green Machine. Parents, friends, and relatives were at the park, as well. We left the park as a group on the bus followed by a load of cars and trucks. Man, I tell you we had so much support our vehicle line was similar to a funeral procession. Riding on the Green Machine is where most of us were introduced to a whole new world of music. Coach wore his shades, Crestwood coaching shirt, shorts, cowboy boots, and hat. Our assistant coaches Tim, Love, Pratt, and Carmichael were also on the bus with us. Mrs. Becky had our game jerseys and pants all nice and neatly folded up at the rear the of the bus. Coach popped in a cassette tape. For the younger generation, cassette tapes were what we had before C.D.'s, Beats by Dre headphones, and YouTube. We heard songs such as Elvis Presley's, *"Blue Suede Shoes"*: You can do anything but stay off of my blue suede shoes.  Yes, I still remember the words.  Also Buddy Holly's, *"Peggy Sue."*:  *Peggy Sue, Peggy Sue, Oh how my heart yearns for you, Oh Peggy.  My Peggy Sue.* Man, when I tell you we had never heard these songs before in the hood.  We were used to *Dumb Girl* by Run D. M. C. and  *5 Minutes of Funk* by Whodini.  But we heard these songs so much you had no choice but to learn them. To be honest, we ended up liking them. It got to a point where we would be singing louder than Coach. You know he got a kick out that.  However, you should have seen the look on the black kids faces when we heard ol Buddy Holly on for the first time. We were looking at each other like what in the world is this. We were trying to figure out how we were supposed to get hype and ready to play listening to this.  Meanwhile, Coach and a few of my white brothers like Wilson, Jeremy, and Charlie were singing and laughing at us. Then, Coach popped in another Elvis Song: *Jailhouse Rock.  "You ain't nothing but a hound dog."* Ladies and gentlemen we were jamming on the bus. Now I have to give it to him because Coach mixed it up a little and hit us with some R&B. Songs like *Caribbean Queen* by Billy Ocean, Tina Turner, *What's Love Got to Do With It*, and Prince, *Lets Go Crazy*.  We also learned songs like Pat Benatar, *We Belong*; Bruce Springsteen, *Dancing in the Dark*; The Police, *Every Breath You Take*; Twisted Sister, *We're Not Going to Take It*; Chicago, *You're My Inspiration*; and Van Halen's, *Jump*.

As we got closer to the field coach Tim and Love would lead us in chants to get us fired up to play. Chants such as the following :

*Lead - And a hottie hottie hottee*
*Team - And a hottie hottie hottee*
*Lead - And a ho ho ho*
*Team - And a ho ho ho*
*Lead - And a skip bop beatle*
*Team - And a skip bop beatle*
*Lead - And a waaaay we go*
*Team - And a waaaay we go*
*Lead - When you see that ball*
*Team - When you see that ball*
*Lead - Going down that field*
*Team - Going down that field*
*Lead - If 22 don't get it*
*Team - If 22 don't get it*
*Lead - Then 32 will*
*Team - Then 32 will*
*And a hottie hottie hottee*

This would repeat with us repeating each player's number at the end. Next, we would start out *Colts get ready to roll Colts get ready to roll (clap clap clap).* We once pulled up to our opponents field and Coach blew this peculiar sounding horn. It was a loud and funny sound, but everyone knew what the sound of the horn meant when they heard it: Coach Daryl's Colts are coming.

We made it to Pinson with the Mom Squad and the entire entourage. We came out strong from the outset of the game with two scores from Andy. Our defense was solid, shutting their offense down the entire game. Cam added two scores and Mike ran for one. The line was dominant as we rolled to a 38-0 victory. Following the game, regardless of the score, Coach only allowed us to say two words to our opponents: "Good Game." Coach taught us that we should always win or lose with class.

We practiced hard in preparation for our week three opponent, the Leeds Greenwaves. They were also 2-0 and had arguably the fastest player in the league at running back. With Coach Love leading the way, our defense took pride in trying to stop their offense. We worked all week in preparing to stop their big, fast running back from getting outside. The red and blue jersey dogfight was at an all-time high. I think Coach sensed the tension between the offense and defense all week. Friday came around, and we were ready to play. After practice, Coach announced that following the game, on the next day, we would be going to Point Mallard Park. Coach and Mrs. Becky helped pick up the tab for the ones who couldn't afford it. We were all excited but had some business to handle first. Leeds came onto our field, and I can remember their huge and tall running back during the weigh-in. They probably were thinking the same thing about our stable of backs. We did a great job on #22 for the most part, but he did get outside once for a long touchdown. We came out victorious with a 28 to 6 win.

After the game, we loaded up the Green Machine and headed to the park. Point Mallard is a waterpark about one hour north of Birmingham in Decatur Alabama; it had several swimming pools, a wave pool, and waterslides. They also had tennis courts, batting cages, and a 3-mile hiking trail. The team moms made us sandwiches and fixed sodas for our lunch. This was a great trip at the perfect time. Our practices with the competition for the green jerseys had become so intense that we seemed like we were two separate teams. The defensive players hated the offenses guys, and the offensive guys hated the defense of players. We needed this trip to bond as a team. There were offensive and defensive players playing on the water slides together. That type of  bonding  was normally only visible on Saturdays, all the other times, we were about the business of football. Coach was on to something because we became closer to each other with this off the field outing.

The following week Coach decided to *Go For Two* in another way. Coach was coming by early on Saturday mornings before games to pick us up on the regular route. So he announced to us that he was not going to be coming around on Saturday mornings anymore. However, everyone on the route could stay at his house on Friday nights. We were all excited to stay and also all players who weighed 72 lbs or higher had to stay as well. Coach was trying to eliminate the running around on Saturday mornings to save time and also to monitor the players whom may have been close to the weight limit. Man, this was an eye-opener for a lot of us. Coach and his wife were opening up their homes to lots of inner-city kids that they only knew a couple of months. The next Friday night after practice we all headed to stay at Coach Daryl house. Growing up in the projects, I had never seen anything like this before. It was at that particular moment, I began to understand that everyone didn't live the same way we did in the inner city. Seeing their home inspired me to do something with my life and listen to what Coach was teaching us about football and life. These Friday nights built another bond with players from different areas and backgrounds. Mrs. Becky, Amy, and Amanda had to be thinking what in the world is Coach doing bringing all these kids into our home. But the Whittington's were a class act, and always showed us love and treated us like we were family. One eye-opener was the cool A/C in the home. Many of us in the projects had those fans in the window to try and keep cool in the summer. The fans had nothing on central air and heat. Also, Coach had a big screen floor model T. V. in the living room. This is where we made pallets and slept. Even now, I'm wondering where did Coach get a big screen from back in 1984. Mrs. Becky would cook us food such as chicken fingers, hamburgers, fries, hot dogs, pizza, and drinks. And if that wasn't enough, we had ice cream and hot fudge sundaes for dessert. I had never seen so much food in my life at one time. I thought the only way you had that much food was at a buffet. Now the players who were 72 lbs or higher had to eat a nice wonderful salad with no desserts. Man, they hated that, but Coach didn't want them to be overweight and not be able to play the next morning. I still say some of the heavyweights may have swiped a chicken finger or two (Munt). The Friday nights stays, we normally played basketball out back, we wrestled and sometimes even boxed against each other. However, it was not all just fun because we use to watch film on our opponents and watch our previous game to critique ourselves. On Saturday mornings, the heavyweights had to eat a light breakfast. Meanwhile, the rest of us had pancakes, eggs, sausages, bacon, waffles and plenty of beverages.

Over the next couple of weeks, we strutted our stuff up and down the field continuing to win each week. The talk was spreading about the undefeated season we were having. We were heading toward the six-week mark at school and in the football season. All of our classmates, especially the ones who played in the Metro League wanted a piece of us. However, Coach wanted a piece of us, but in a different way. At the six week mark is where we received our report cards. Coach requested for all of us to bring our report cards to practice when we received them. See Coach not only wanted us to be successful on the field, but he also wanted us to be successful in the classroom. Everyone with bad grades, such as a D or F had to answer to him. And any player with a C, D, or F in conduct had to answer to Coach as well. Yes, for the younger generation, we had conduct grades in school. Coach always said that everyone might not be an honor roll student. However, each one of us can act right, listen, and respect the teachers. Coach worked on getting help for kids with failing grades, but the players with bad conduct, Coach, gave them extra running at practice. Yes, even a C in conduct was not good enough. Coach felt that was not good enough for self- behavior. If you received a D or F in conduct, not only was it extra running in practice, but you would get a visit from Coach at your school. He was very concerned about us as kids, and not just football players.

So we continued our winning streak and went on to become 9-0 with one more regular season game. This would be "The game of the year.": Crestwood versus Central Park. This was the team who won the AYFL championship the previous year and was number one in the league. They were very good and led by one of the best running backs in the league, Cedric Sparks. The practice was as intense as ever, in order to have a chance to win, we knew stopping Sparks was key. The battle for the green jerseys was furious. Two weeks prior we had gotten our guard Mauricus back from his collarbone injury, which was just in time for this matchup. Coach Tim and Coach Love had our offense and defense ready. Friday night came around, and we all went over to Coach's house to spend the night. This particular night it was less playing around and more film watching. Again as I stated, Mike and Andy's dad used to film ours and our opponents games. So while we were watching Central Park, we saw that Sparks ran the ball a lot and he was very fast and elusive. Playing defensive end myself and Reginald knew that this task would be huge.

So Saturday morning comes, and we get ready to head to the ballpark. Upon arriving, Coach made sure all of the heavyweights were 75 lbs or less. At the park, we met the rest of the team and all loaded up on the Green Machine to head to Central Park. The bus was followed by our fans and families. Central Park's games were played on a baseball field. They were blue and gold and located near the Alabama State Fairgrounds, which is now known as the Crossplex. So we arrived, and it's people everywhere. We could see kids out running telling others we were about to turn in. Coach hits the famous horn as we pull in chanting Colts get ready to roll Colts get ready to roll (clap clap clap). Our fans are cheering us on and ready. Their fans were doing a lot of talking and had lots of swagger, and for good reason. They are the defending champs and are undefeated as well. Everyone on our team made the weigh-in, so we were good. Coach never allowed one of our opponents kids not to play because of being overweight. He always allowed every player to play, no matter what. Can't say that for our opposing coaches. If one of our players was over by half of a pound, the answer was always no. But hey, those were the rules of the league. The opposing coaches weighed you and made the call.

So the game starts, the crowd is loud, and it seems as if there is no room anywhere, not even to stand. The older pounds also came to the field at 10:30 to see this one. We came out on defense first as usual and stopped them on their first couple of possessions. They were up for the challenge by stopping us also. The score broke when we fumbled the ball which they picked up and ran it in for a score. They converted to two-point conversion to take the lead 8-0. We battle back with a long drive capped off by a 30 yard run from Andy. We converted our two point conversion which left the score 8-8. The game went back and forth with both fans basis yelling, cheering and running up and down the field. They scored two more times but we held them on the extra points leaving the score 20-8. We scored on a run from Mike to make the game 20-14. Cam got the two point try to make it 20-16. This was the score late in the fourth quarter. We got a huge stop on defense which gave us the ball back. We had the ball last with under two minutes remaining. We managed to get to their 35-yard-line with only seconds remaining. Coach called a timeout, and it didn't look good for us. We needed a pass which there weren't many completed all year. I was not in the huddle when Coach called the play, but Wilson said it was a double reverse. Both teams had played their hearts out. Our Mom Squad and fans looked on nervously. Next, the offense ran back on the field. I'm on one knee looking on. While in the huddle, Wilson decides to change the play. He thought with only a short amount of time remaining that we needed a pass play. Wilson swapped with James and played the center position and James went to quarterback. Plus, Wilson knew James could throw the ball into the end zone from where we were located. They change the play to the Saffo bomb. Both of our receivers To-Jo and Terrail last names were Saffo, so we had a play that they both ran straight down the field called the Saffo bomb. So Wilson lined up at center and James went under center to take the snap. Coach didn't know what was going on, but the look on his face when James drop back to pass was like "Imma kill Wilson!" Terrail and To Jo went deep, and I think it caught Central Park off guard because it was our only pass attempt of the game. James launches a rocket in the air. Man, it seemed like the ball was in the air forever. To-Jo went up and came down with the catch in the end zone for a win of 22-20. Our fans went crazy, and we went crazy, and the coaches went crazy. So here we are one year removed from being one of the worst teams in the league to being undefeated regular season champs. All you could hear from us and our fans was *"Who dat talking bout beating the Colts, who dat who dat, say what."* Central Park was a tough team that was definetly going to have something to say during the playoffs.

Despite going undefeated during regular season it's now playoff time and everyone was focused. Our goal was to be the AYFL League Champs. Coach came to practice the following Monday like we were 0-10. He kept telling us that this is a new season and despite being undefeated, one loss and it's over. The fight for the green jerseys again was a battle. Our first round opponent was going to be against Huffman. They were orange and green and reminded you of the Miami Hurricanes. This team was good and had a lot of athletes. Gameday came, and we took care of business. Huffman played tough, but we prevailed with a win of 26-0. After this game we had to make an adjustment at practice. Our park didn't have any lights so after daylight savings time; we had to switch fields and practice at Avondale Park. This was a baseball park approximately 5 min down the road. Also after the 1st round, all of the pounds were cut down from not making it or winning. It was only our pound and our 95 lb remaining. This also meant we had more field to utilize at practice. The semifinal matchup was against Leeds. We watched the film from our game earlier in the season on stopping their #22. Coach Love game plan was for us to gang tackle their big fast back and to by no means let him outside. We ran drills in the open field tackling from the outside in and not the inside out. We wanted to push him toward the middle of our defense. Leeds come to town the next sat with a lot of hype and for good reason. Early in the first quarter their star back got loose on a 40 yard run and we went down 6-0. Coach Love and Daryl both lit into us on defense about that. But after that we woke up and shut him down the rest of the game. The defense again was solid led by Reg, To-Jo and Quincy. Andy ran for two scores, Mike,Cam, and Randy ran for one as we rolled to a 38-6 semifinal victory. This would send us to our first AYFL championship and guess who was awaiting the Colts. You got it. The defending champs Central Park. The next week was a peculiar week of practice because for the first time all year we had the entire field to ourselves. We were the only pound that made it to the finals. We knew a battle was ahead of us to dethrone the previous champions. To be the best you have to beat the best. We worked on angles to the ball and plays that we messed up on a couple of weeks prior. We had a great week of practice and were ready for our first finals game. Friday night we migrated over to Coach's home. After arriving we ate, played games, and watch the film from our previous game with Central Park. On Saturday morning we got up and headed to our ballpark. We met the rest of our teammates and loaded up on the bus. Our fans lined up behind us on the way to the finals. All of the finals were held at Lawson field. The field is located about five minutes away from our park. This is also where a lot of high school football games were played. For this to be a youth league game it had the feeling of a high school or college rivalry. One side blue and gold and the other green and white. The field was packed with support from all of the other pounds, friends and family. We came out fast with scores from Mike, Cam and Randy. Our defense was stellar this time, holding their running back to minimum yardage. Andy also scored twice to cap the game off. This time we didn't need a hailmary pass to win. We ran away with the title 36-6. We were the AYFL 75 lb undefeated League Champs. Man, what a feeling to work so hard, and finally get to celebrate our accomplishment. What a turnaround under Coach Daryl and assistants Love, Tim, Pratt, and Carmichael. Our assistants were such a vital part of our learning and getting us ready to play week in and week out. As we left the field, the Mom Squad, cheerleaders, friends, and family all were there to greet us. Everyone chanting *"Who dat talking bout beating them Colts who dat who dat say what."* Also as we left the field, the tenacious mom squad was chanting, *"We are proud of you, and we are proud of you (clap clap clap)."* Coach had something for us back on the bus. He congratulated us on our season and gave us what we thought were individual champagne bottles. We were chanting and pouring the drinks on each other and just knew we were drunk. In all essence, we were drinking Welch's grape juice. But to us it was some nice, cold, good ol champagne.

We ended the season with our banquet where we received trophies and awards. Coach also explained to us that at any moment the ball could have bounced in a different direction and we could lose. He stated that this football (holding up a ball) has a funny bounce to it. He said that if he drops the ball that he was holding several times that each time it would roll to a different position before stopping. The message was you never know what can happen in a football game. He had that same message before each game during the season. He said that the key was to make sure you work hard and prepare to win. He always told us that everyone has the will to win; however, everyone won't have the will to prepare to win. This is so true because everyone wants money and success, but everyone doesn't want to put in the work and preparation to get it. Coach informed us that the next season would be different, and now the target will be on our backs. He said we have to man up, accept the challenge and get ready to work our tail off.

Now that the remarkable first 13-0 undefeated 75lb season is now over. Lets roll over to chapter three to see what happens in the second season with the 85 lb Coach Daryl's Crestwood Colts.

**Crestwood Colts 75 lbTeam**

## Chapter 3
## The 85 LB

With our first season in the books with an impressive 13-0 record, Coach Daryl's team was riding high. We took our swag and bragging rights back to school with us. The word was out about our undefeated season. Meanwhile, a lot of our classmates wasn't buying the hype. Some of my buddies who played in the Metro league claimed that we didn't play any tough teams. My friends played with teams such as Eastlake Cowboys, Ensley Broncos, and A. G. Gaston Boys Club. We couldn't even enjoy our perfect season without a little hate. This goes to show you, whenever you are successful, there will be people who don't like it. They had no idea of the hard work we put in all season. They underestimated some the teams that played in our league. All of this talk really made us angry and ready to begin the next season more determined than ever. However, it seems time passed slowly between late November and the start of July before we could get back to practice. Living in the projects made time seemed to past even slower. Too much idle time and plenty of opportunities to do wrong. Coach Daryl had to be thinking of us and how he could keep us out of the streets and out of trouble.

February 1985, I received a call from Coach asking if I would be interested in playing baseball. Of course, the answer was a no-brainer. In Kingston we played basketball, baseball, and football all year round. We had a few of the players come out such as Wilson, Cam, myself, Randy, Mauricus (Dale Murphy) James, Andy, Reg, To-Jo, Terrail, and Quincy. We practiced at Avondale Park which was the same place our football practices were held toward the end of the season. Playing baseball was definitely going to keep us busy and away from other things we could have been doing. We didn't have a clue on how things would turn out, but to our surprise, the season went great. At an early age, guys like Andy and James were good at baseball. Coach took plenty of time with us teaching the fundamentals of baseball. We picked it up well and won all of our games and the championship. We had so much fun and became closer as a team. Unfortunately, right after the season, we were asked not to come back again. I guess the league said we were like the modern day Kentucky Basketball (one and done). But overall this was another bonding period and a great experience.

When school let out, we had begun to enjoy our 1985 summer break. It didn't take long for June to come and everyone is signing up for football, again. Coach calls the team asking for our participation to put in work for a fundraiser for the team. The money raised would help us purchase new uniforms. We were all in with this idea. The next Saturday we met at Crestwood Park, hopped on the Green Machine, and headed up the road to Century Plaza Mall. Century Plaza Mall was the spot where everyone went to shop and hang out. The mall, surrounded by several eating places, and stores was adjacent to another mall called Eastwood. The intersection between the two malls were very busy, especially on Saturdays. Once we arrived coach parked the bus in one of the parking lots and gave us our instructions. We were wearing our green and white t-shirts and shorts so we could all be easily identified as being together. The first topic of instruction was safety. For the fundraiser, we had to ask people in cars for donations at the red lights. Our schedule went as follows: start asking for donations early morning, take breaks, take a lunch, and take an afternoon break later that evening. We finished up later after the evening break. Coach told us to make sure we have each other's back and to look out for one another. He also mentioned to never go out while the light was green and cars were moving. We had to always travel in pairs so that one person can ask for donations while your partner watched the opposite light. When the opposite light turned yellow, that was the signal to get back on the median. After that, Coach informed us to be polite and ask for the donation. He warned us that some people would not support our cause but just merely respond by saying thank you. Something else that Coach wanted us to be aware of was that some people may not take too well to black kids coming up to their vehicles. He said that some might roll their windows up, clutch their purses, or say mean words and may even call us the "N" word. Nevertheless he told us just respond by saying thank you. So we go out and in groups on the main intersection off of Crestwood Blvd and Oporto Madrid Street. It is sad to say, but things took place just as Coach stated. There were lots of people who gave and supported us. However, a few people did roll their windows up, grabbed their purses and even called us the "N" word. Some of our white teammates were in shock. They couldn't believe that people would say things of that nature to kids. Halfway through the day, the Mom Squad made us sandwiches and gave us juices to help us cool down. We worked the rest of the afternoon and had a very productive fundraiser. Some of the money from the fundraiser helped the kids on our team with their league fee. Some of us couldn't afford the $50 cost. Coach helped pay for a few players to play the previous year. Yes, it was only $50 to play football. Man, what happened to those days.

July 1985, the park started football practices at the field for all of the teams. Feeling ourselves, more than a little, due to having two pounds now smaller than us being the

65 lb and 75 lb. The three pounds above us were the 95 lb, 105 lb, and the largest pound the 115 lb. The larger pound teams seemed like giants to us. All of the pounds knew about Coach Daryl and our undefeated season. The rest of our league and other leagues knew of us and the Big Green Machine. We had players from everywhere that came out for tryouts. I did say tryouts, because that's exactly what it felt like to make our team. There had to be over 70 guys on the first day of practice. It didn't take long for Coach Daryl and his crew to ramp up. As soon as some of the guys got a day of our coaches hardcore, in your face, approach, the number of players took a nose dive. The twenty-five or so guys from the previous 75 lb team had seen this scenario play out before. Some players just couldn't handle the running and fiery coaches. There were some parents who told Coach what position their child played, and basically, wanted Coach to place their son in that position on the team. Coach told the parents that all positions were open and that each player would be given an opportunity, However, nothing was guaranteed. This made some parents angry and upset. Some said things to Coach like "who do you think you are? If I pay my $50 my son is gonna play." Coach told parents that he had approximately 25 players returning and those 25 would all remain a part of the team. He said we only have around 40 jerseys, so not many more boys can be added. Coach was loyal to all of us; even if it was a second or third string player. Once on the team, you were not losing your spot for no one. Some of these parents removed their kids and went elsewhere. One thing about our parents; they allowed Coach and the assistants to Coach us, and they stayed on the sidelines. Even when we were getting chewed out. I don't believe our parents got in the way at all with our coaches. They all knew that coach had every

child's heart at hand and he wanted the best for all of us. Despite all of the players who left and did not make it, some guys endured the practices and made the team: Horace Burgess (Chubb), Verdell Snider (Big Dog), Quantell Harold, Marcus Henry, Jeff Wildermuth, and Calvin Patton all came aboard.

Each year we had open tryouts for all positions. Each year players grew significantly, and their bodies changed over time. Always try kids in different areas each year, because you never know where they will excel. I know first hand because Verdell came in and won my previous position at defensive end and moved me to corner. Chubb came in and won a safety spot and second string running back. Quantell contributed at defensive back. Calvin had playing time on the defensive line. Jeff came along to play center and offensive line. Now the 85 lb team began to formulate and we worked every player into first, second and third string. The depth we had at multiple positions was a huge part of our success. If we got up by two or more scores, Coach would not allow you to go back in the game at your starting position, because of this, guys had to be skilled at multiple positions. And this was one way of getting extra playing time. Guys did not make a fuss about where they played. You had running backs going to Coach Love to get in as a defensive lineman. We would play anywhere to get back in the game. It could be on the kickoff team, return team, it did not matter. Defensive players were going on the offensive sides trying to block, all for more reps. This really made our whole team better, because if one person was out, we really didn't miss a beat.

By this time our jerseys had come in, and wow they were the best. All of the other Crestwood teams had only one uniform, which was the plain, white jerseys with Crestwood written in green across the front with the numbers in the front and back in green. We had home jerseys and away jerseys. Our jerseys were different across the shoulder pads. The white jerseys had green on top with white numbers on them. Our sleeves also had green and whites stripes. Our green jerseys were just the opposite. We typically wore green tops with white pants and the white jerseys with green pants. Coach brought us some socks that were green at the top and white on the bottom. With every player dressed the same, we took the field like an NFL team.

So as we prepared for the new season and the talk from our friends continued to grow. We were the target, just as coach had told us. The teams from the metro league were all calling. Coach accepted one of the invites, and we took the Green Machine down Hwy 59 south to play the Ensley Broncos. Their players had been saying they would beat us, and now it was time to see. When we arrived at their field, located between downtown Birmingham and Bessemer, AL, Coach hit the horn of the famous Green Machine. People were everywhere talking all kinds of trash. Just before the weigh-in, Coach tells the Ensley coach, "Don't worry about the checking the player's weight, we just want to play." They went into their field house and came back out ready to play. The game starts, and it is a back and forth early on. We were stopping them, and they were stopping us; getting into our backfield on almost every play. Coach became livid at our offensive line about their blocking. After Andy scored on a long run, we went into halftime up 7-0. Defensively we held our own the entire game, by not giving up a single point. We continued to struggle a little on offense but managed to take the win 21-0. Cam scored on a reverse and Randy took one to the house. After the game, our coaches were trying to understand why we had so much trouble moving the ball on offense. When we came back to practice and watched the film, we found that Ensley had 12 men on the field the entire game on defense and we never recognized it. All of our coaches apologized to the team, and especially our offensive line for getting on them so hard during the game. This win gave us bragging rights back at school. One of their players attended my school. He made all sorts of excuses for losing against us. He also lived across the street from my apartment. It took years for him to fess up, but he finally told me some wild news. He said that after our coach decided not to weigh in that day, their coach added some players from their 95lb to help try and beat us. Another lesson learned right here. Whenever you are successful, people will try and do anything to bring you down. The attempt did not work for them. The 85lb team was off to a 1-0 start.

Back at practice, we worked would on fundamentals and battled each other. After a couple of days, Coach accepted another scrimmage from the so-called best Metro League team: A. G. Gaston. They had a great program, and their 85 lb team had a claim of being the best in their league. Ensley, too, had claimed to be the best. This time we were playing at our field. Most of our other pounds ended their practice early and watched. We had the 50-yard line to the end zone to scrimmage. A. G. Gaston showed up with more players than us. They had their all-white jerseys with blue stripes and white pants. Of course, Coach Daryl didn't make them weigh-in. So both teams agreed to the game rules. They were to go on offense with a 30-minute running clock. Each time they scored, or each time we stopped them from scoring they had to start back at the 50-yard line. Interceptions and fumbles also would re-start the drive. They would run as many possessions as possible in those 30 minutes. After that, we would swap and go on offense placing the same 30-minute running clock on the scoreboard and get as many drives as we could.  They got the ball first, and we stopped them on their first drive.  Key defensive plays were carried out by Dewayne, To-Jo, Verdell, Reg, Chubb, and myself.  The next drive, A. G. Gaston went down and scored and got the two-point conversion. The score was A. G. Gaston 8 and Crestwood 0.  The crowd is going crazy.  They knew that we had just finished off an undefeated season as well. Now after the touchdown, there was about 26 minutes left on the clock for them to play offense. They had about 10-12 more starting drives in that time frame. Our defense locked down, and they did get into the end zone again. Regardless of attempts, they didn't get many 1st downs after the scoring drive.  Coach Love and Coach Daryl gave it to us after giving up that score. Charles and Cam had some nice pass breakups on defense.  Next A.G. Gaston 30 minutes ran out, and now we swap to play offense. I took my helmet off to watch the rest of the game. It's now around 7:20 - 7:25 in which it starts to get dark around 8 pm in July.  On our first offensive possession, we go right down the field and score.  Andy scores on a 12-yard run dragging a couple of their players in the end zone.  Mike scores the two-point conversion to tie the game at 8-8. There are about 28 minutes still left on the board, and our fans are excited. A,G. went to the sideline knowing that they couldn't stop us and their coach decided to leave. He claimed that it was too dark at 7:25 to continue to play. He said that his players couldn't see.  Now there is plenty of daylight remaining, almost 30 minutes worth.  Everyone knew that we didn't have field lights, so they used it as an excuse. They walked off our field and took their uniforms off. They didn't shake our hands or anything. They got back on their bus and left.  We tried to play the game several more times but never received a return call from them. Coach offered to play at their field, but they never took the offer.

Going into our second season, we were ready. This defense was nasty. We gang tackled and tried not to give up any yards. Some may argue that the Tampa two defense was made famous by players like Derrick Brooks, Warren Sapp, and John Lynch from the Tampa Bay Buccaneers; however, the Colts were playing it back in 1985. Our outstanding running back stable had a total of six backs that could have started for any team in the league. Also, Wilson and James were passing the ball more to To-Jo and Terrail. The starting backfield stood as Andy, Mike, and Cam. The explosive Randy, Chubb, and T.J. continued the second team backfield. Charles and I were second-string receivers. Jeff, T.J., Mauricus, Demetrius, and Reg continued to play a strong offensive line.

We gave it our all. Our first regular season game was against Leeds. Reg and Verdell had been working hard all week on making sure they were disciplined at defensive ends. The entire defense was up for the challenge of stopping the great back on the Leeds team. Our battle for the green jerseys continued. We were all fired to play the start of the season game against Leeds. Our defense came out and stopped them on their first drive. Our offense was sharp and clicking on all cylinders. We scored on our first three drives to jump out on the green waves. We continue to gang tackle their backs, which gave them all kinds of problems. Our offense continued to dominate, scoring a total of 36 points. We gave up one score at the end of the game. The final score was 36-6. Winning against Leeds, was a great way to start the 85 lb season.

We moved on to week two and faced a tough ballgame against Huffman; we battled for four quarters. We were solid in all three phases of the game. Huffman gave us a great ball game, but we managed to pull out the win, 22-0.

After Huffman, our next opponent was East Walker. We didn't play against this team the previous season, so our coaches weren't familiar with them. We heard that they threw the ball most of the time. Playing corner was great news for me. It was game time, and we were ready for the battle. Mike led the way with two touchdowns. Chubb, Randy, T.J, and Cam ran for one. Dewayne and To-Jo led the team in tackles. I had two picks, and Chubb picked one. They did get two passing touchdowns against us in the second half. The final score ended up 50-12.

Back at practice, we worked on our passing defense, since we gave up those two touchdowns. Coach Love was not happy about those 12 points. We worked on a bunch of tip drills and taking the correct angles in covering receivers. Our offense was in full stride as we prepared for our next game against Pelham. The defense got it back together in this game shutting down any attempt they had to score points. Munt, Jeremy, and Charley led the defense. On offense, Andy scored two; James and Wilson threw touchdowns to Terrail and ToJo; Randy also scored on a 50-yard run. The final score was 36-0.

We moved on to our next opponent for the season, and that was the Tarrant Wildcats. This game was a little different because they had been talking trash all week about ending our little winning streak. Their coach also told everyone that we weren't that good. I guess he was trying to pump his team up, but he was only ticking off Coach Daryl. A strange relationship developed between Coach Daryl and the Tarrant coach. We didn't know much about this team. After the long and hard week of practice, we headed to their field for the matchup. Doing the weigh-in before the game, all of their players and coaches were yelling and talking trash to us. Coach Love told us privately that if they scored a touchdown on our defense that we would have hell to pay come Monday. Coach Daryl commanded us to not say anything back to them but to do all of our talking with our pads. I think they were attempting to intimidate us. Coach had never allowed us to run the score up on anyone, until this point. He would always played the second and third string if we got up by two or more scores. Since they were talking so much crap, he made an exception to the Tarrant game, as opposed to all other games. We took care of business and won by the score of 50-0. After the game, coach made sure that none of us said anything to them besides good game. Coach use to tell us before every game that the football has a funny bounce to it. Also on any given Saturday, the ball may not bounce our way. So if we win or lose, Coach taught us always to do it with class.

After we beat Tarrant, then there was the Fultondale game. We continued our home pre-game introductions which were always cool. Each player running out as their name and number was called, gave everyone a sense of pride. Every game we played brought large crowds from all over the place. Everyone wanted to see Coach Daryl's Colts. No matter who the opponent was, people were coming to see us play. The game against Fultondale would not be any different. We continue to roll to a 34-0 victory.

Our next victim would come in a thrashing victory over Trussville. The score got out of hand and ended up being 56-0. Many of the second and third string players played most of the game. After the first quarter, nobody went back in the game at their starting position; we were taught to play multiple positions; this gave the coaches flexibility and gave the team depth in case of an injury. Knowing multiple positions was also the only way you were put back in the game, at all, if we were up a couple of scores.

During the next week of practice coach set up a scrimmage against our 95 lb team. They were bigger than us and also a good team. They ran a power wishbone offense. They were led by their talented fullback Lorenzo Ford. He was big, fast and a load to bring down. I always got a kick out of tackling him because Lorenzo was my best friend. As you know on the football field, none of that matters. We held up pretty well against them; however, no one kept score. Coach probably designed that scrimmage at the right time, because our next game was against the AYFL runner-ups for the 75 lb teams: Central Park. This particular game against Central Park would be a home game for us. Their fans came in droves, seeking revenge from the previous year championship game. Their talented back averaged over 100 yards rushing, and a couple of scores per game. Coach Love and Pratt had the defense ready for the challenge. Coach Daryl and Tim had the offense locked and loaded. Our fans were eager, and the park was extremely packed. The game stars and our defense came out first, as usual, dominating. We held their back to 40 yards on over 20 carries in the ball game. We were hitting him hard the whole game. However, he slipped into the end zone, once toward the end the game on a reverse. Seeing that official hold up the touchdown sign, was something we didn't like and something we did not want to see again. Mike, Cam, Andy, and Randy all took runs to the house. The final score was 36-6

Now we are at our last regular season game, and for some reason, we played Leeds again. We took the Green Machine up Hwy 20, northbound to their field. Their colors were also green and white. Once again, we had planned to keep their back in the middle of the field and contain him. He was more massive than anyone on our defense. I can remember ToJo and Dwayne walloped him after Reg pushed him back inside. We heard a few sniffles, and that was all she wrote. The defense pitched another shutout with the score of 50-0. The Colts were still rolling. On offense, Randy and Cam scored twice. T.J and Chubb scored once. We were playing the best football and heading toward the tournament.

The playoffs came in which only the top eight teams were playing. We were the number one seed, and we drew Pinson in the first round. We continued to brawl at practice for the green jerseys and prepared to make a run at the repeat. On the first round game, all three phases of the game were on point: the offense, defense, and special teams. Cam took a kickoff to the house behind our wall play; we practiced this all year long and finally got one for a score. We set the wall up to come on our sideline with TJ and ToJo coming to the opposite direction, hitting anyone trying to make the tackle. Coach enjoyed seeing us execute the play to perfection. The final score was 38-0.

The semifinal matchups were now all set up. We played South Roebuck, and Center Point played Central Park. Center Point won their game and awaited the winner of our game. South Roebuck was a team who loved to throw the ball and had a good quarterback with a strong arm. They also had some good receivers. We continued our domination with Andy scoring two touchdowns. Wilson ran in a quarterback sneak. James hit Terrail for a 35-yard pass to score. Mike and Cam also scored one. Reg, James and T J led the team in tackles. I had an interception and Randy recovered a fumble. Our offensive line was stellar, opening up holes behind Mauricus, T.J. Reg, Mete, and Jeff. The final score in the semis was 44-0.

The finals arrived and we are gearing up for our second consecutive championship appearance. Center Point, an excellent team, had only one loss in the season. We continued to battle each other in practice, trying to win the green jerseys. Repetition of what we had done all season was the key. We didn't change anything up but we had a few wrinkles up our sleeve if needed. Gameday arrives; we load into the Green Machine at our park. Just like the previous year, the finals were held at Lawson field. We grandly arrived with our usual rituals, followed by a load of cars. There was always at least 40 cars behind the bus. Coach sounds the horn to let everyone know that we were officially there; It was always fun and exciting seeing everyone's head turn and look at us as we pulled up. Center Point also brought a great crowd. Once we exited the bus, in a single filed line, we entered the field. In the locker room, Coach gave us our normal pre-game speech. He always told us that if the ball didn't bounce our way, to make sure we showed good sportsmanship by only saying to our opponent "good game." Both teams came out a little sluggish, but we managed to take a 12-0 lead to the half. Coach and our assistant coaches came down on us at halftime about playing not to lose. I guess you can say we got their message. We continued to dominate both lines of scrimmage and won the game 34-0. Wow, two years in a row we were back to back undefeated AYFL champions. For the second year in a row, we celebrated by popping our champagne/Welch's grape juice bottles. Our fans were elated. Some of the gangsters from our neighborhoods congratulated us. Coming off the field, our cheerleader, parents, fans, all greeted us. This win was a wonderful feeling for the green and white Crestwood Colts. The famous Mom Squad led the cheers singing, "We are proud of you, and we are proud of you (clap, clap, clap)."

Sometimes just having someone in your corner can make all the difference in a kid's life. It was the most indescribable feeling, seeing all those smiling faces and hearing all of the cheers. Once we settled down, Coach made an announcement that we had been invited to Florida to play in the Miracle Strip Bowl. We all went nuts; the team was beyond excited. For some players, including myself, this would be our first time out of the state of Alabama. So instead of ending the season, we headed back to practice for: Can you say, "ROAD TRIP."

We had few practice sessions and prepared to test our team against others from all over the Southeast. Coach Daryl had no clue who we were supposed to play and no information about the teams. The only thing we knew was that eight teams were invited. These teams were also league champs from their states. It was now the week of Thanksgiving in November 1985, and the Green Machine is at our park gassed up and ready to roll. All of our coaches, parents, the Mom Squad, cheerleaders, and fans were locked and loaded. A fitting song played on the radio, Van Halen's, "Panama." The team laughed, joked, and sang all the way down there. Our team moms Mrs. Whittington, Mrs. Rice, and Mrs. Thomas made sandwiches for us to eat while traveling. I can't say enough about Mrs. Becky. Besides washing our practice and game uniforms, she cooked plenty of food for everyone when we spent the night at their home. She did all of these things while working and taking care of her kids.Looking back, I don't know how she did it. I do know that behind every great man, there is a magnificent woman behind the scenes making things happen. When I asked her how she did it, Mrs. B said that she was running around "crazy as hell." She also loved the fact that she endured it all. Mrs. Becky told me that there were times when quitting came to her mind. She said that at those moments, Coach Daryl talked her out of it, and would say, "Becky we are doing this for the boys." After Coach's encouragement, her answer would always be "Ok Daryl." Because of your dedication and sacrifice, from all of the boys, we want to say, "We Love You, Mrs. Becky."

Arriving at Panama City, Florida, we were looking wide-eyed at the awesome beaches and the unique palm trees. Man, we had never seen anything like that before in our lives. We couldn't wait to get out there and have some fun in the sun. We checked into Tourway Inn, located right on the beach. Upon opening the hotel doors, within a few steps, our feet were in the sand. Before everyone dispersed, Coach met with us to go over some house rules. Coach Daryl, a strict disciplinarian, did not play the radio (play around). He told us to be on our best behavior, look out for each other, and if anyone got out of line, they would have to deal with him. After Coach laid down the rules, he did something that shocked us all; Coach passed out room assignments and keys. We were all on the same row, upstairs and downstairs. Keep in mind that we are the 85 lb team, so most of the players were ages seven, eight, and nine-years-old. We were assigned four players to each room without the parents. One player would be the captain and the leader of the room. The leader took responsibility for the players in his room making it to meetings, getting to meals, and getting to practice on time. Coach used these type of situations to teach us to be disciplined in life, just like we were on the field. All of the players rooms were in the middle of the hotel row with the coaches rooms on the end. The Mom Squad, parents, and cheerleaders were in the rooms above us. We hit the beach playing football in the sand: this was like heaven on earth. Our football games in the sand were a sight to see: all sorts of players playing wishful positions. Sparkplug, the noseman, played quarterback in the sand, repeating our quarterback call, "Ready, team down, sed hike!" We always got to the line of scrimmage getting our distance six inches apart from one another. In every game, when the quarterback yelled ready, the offensive lineman would all, simultaneously, hit their thigh pads once with both hands. Then the quarterback would say, "Team down!" which meant every lineman stood straight up and then back down to a three-point stance; this was followed by "sed- hike." This significant quarterback call was unique to our team; I never saw anyone doing it back then, and I still haven't seen it this day. We finished up outside play and retired to the rooms. We played and went in and out of each other's room all night. The rooms were adjoined, so if not locked, you could go into your next door neighbor's room, from yours. We were all kids having a great time. The following morning we were to be up for breakfast by 8 am. All room captains had to get their roommates up and out on time. Since I was chosen as one of the leaders, my mom would call about 7 am every morning. She would say, "Corey, are y'all awake down there?" I would respond by saying yes, knowing that we were all knocked out. Truthfully, we probably had just gone to sleep after 3 am. After a couple of mornings when the phone rang, all of the guys would say, "Corey, it's your mom." I guess moms will always be moms. Despite supposively having the 8 am breakfast time, the real start time was always bout an hour later. I think Coach knew that we were not going to be ready, but he was trying to teach us time and responsibility. On Thanksgiving day we ate breakfast, had a small practice on the beach, and finally finished the day with more fun at the beach.

On Friday, game day finally arrived. We all loaded up on the bus to head toward the field. After reaching the field, Coach sounded off the famous horn. Ironically, we didn't know anything about the other teams, but somehow, everyone knew of us. We came out and took care of business against a team named Melville; 34-0. We dominated the game from start to finish. After the ballgame, we arrived back at the hotel and saw the strangest but the most exciting thing on television: Ourselves! Yes, the news had our highlights of the game on T. V. We were overjoyed to see ourselves; however, they were labeling us as some bad guys. James had a cast on his arm from having a broken bone, but he still managed to play. The news said it was an illegal arm wrapping. They also said things like we were too old and cheaters. Now you are talking about a team coached by a man full of nothing but integrity. Coach Daryl would never use a player that was too old or overweight, and he especially would not have allowed us to utilize anything illegal. It was fantastic to see ourselves on the news, but not in this manner. Despite the bad mouthing of the Florida news station, we stayed focus and moved on to the semifinal game the next day.

The semifinal game was against, Cedar Grove, a team we had seen play the previous day; they were outstanding. They were larger than us and had plenty of talent. They were also some undefeated league champs, and we could see why. The game went back and forth, but we could not get into the end zone: we fumbled, had mental breakdowns, or something would happen to stop us. Giving them their due credit, let's just say they were a great team, too. Could this be the game coach kept talking about; where the ball is not going to bounce our way. At half-time, the score was 0-0. The third quarter was more of the same lots of hard hitting and hard nose football with no scoring. Both of our teams had stellar defenses. At the end of the third quarter, the score remained 0-0. Our fans were cheering but concerned at this point. Finally, late in the 4th quarter, Andy broke loose for a 30-yard touchdown and Mike ran the two-point conversion in to put us up 8-0. Our defense held on their last attempt to score and secure the win 8-0. In this tough, hard-fought, battle we were able to walk away with a win.

After our game, we headed back to the hotel to watch the Alabama vs. Auburn, the 1985 Iron Bowl. Being from Alabama, college football has always been huge. And there is no game bigger than this one. Unbelievably, we were from Birmingham, but we were one day away from playing in the finals in Florida. Meanwhile, the Iron Bowl is about to kickoff at Legion Field in Birmingham. We all took our showers and met in one room to watch the game. The room split; some of us for Auburn, and the others for Bama. The '85 Iron Bowl was nothing short of a classic battle. They went back and forth with both fan bases thinking they were going to win. Late in the game, Gene Jelks scored on a play that put Bama up 22-16. The Bama fans in the room are going crazy and jumping all on other players and the beds. Then Reggie Ware scored for Auburn. However, Auburn missed their two-point conversion attempt. This left the score at 23-22 Auburn's way. At the end of the game, Alabama took a sack but came back, completed a long pass to about the 35-yard line of Auburn. Next, Van Tiffin comes out to try for the game-winner. For the first time, during the entire game, there was silence from almost 40 guys. The kick goes up and in, and Bama wins 25-23. The Bama fans in the room are screaming, yelling and going crazy. This 25-23 win is just one of the reasons the Alabama and Auburn game is the best rivalry in college football. No offense to my Michigan and Ohio State fans.

Later that night, Coach decided to take us to the movies, before we played for the championship the next day. We found out that our opponent was going to be Drummond Park. They were another undefeated team and was supposed to be the best team in the tournament. The movie choice for that evening was Rocky IV. The movie paralleled what we were about to face. Rocky had to go into the enemy's territory in Russia to fight. This championship game in Florida was our Russia. We were the underdogs playing in our opponent's backyard. We had to take on the attitude of Rocky and be laser focus for the task at hand. I can remember all of our eyes being wide-open throughout the movie. The battle in Russia took place, and Rocky was losing, but he persevered to come back to win the fight. This type of perseverance can be illustrated in football and in life. Whenever it appears that you are facing defeat, you should dig down deep and continue to fight. When Rocky picked up the Russian and dumped him on the canvas, all of us jumped out of our seats; Verdell knocked my popcorn right out of my hand. Rocky IV has always been my all-time favorite movie. I can't tell you how many times I have watched it. Even today I can sit down and watch it just like it was November 1985. This movie had such an impact on me that I have never watched Rocky V; don't ask why, but it all ended with me in Russia.

The next day, we were face-to-face with the finals. We got up, left the hotel, and headed to the field. We are all Rocky laser focused and ready to roll. The field is packed, and the crowd is loud. Our fans dressed in their green and white were both excited and nervous. Drummond Park, the team we were playing, like us, had never lost a game in two years. They were talented, but their talent would not be enough on this day. Our defense, stout, kept them out of the end zone the entire game. The offense got rolling and racked up 28 points. After the game, these guys didn't even shake our hands. They left the field with seconds remaining. Despite our opponents, we still celebrated with class. Our fans were elated, and we were again champions.

Our annual banquet was held a couple of weeks later back in Birmingham. Upon our return, the word was all over town about our championship win in Florida. We received awards, trophies and a plaque. Coach congratulated us on our success over the past two seasons. We had accomplished our goal; we were champions. He also warned us about becoming complacent and losing our competitive edge. Coach informed us that every team we play would give us their best effort week in and week out. He talked about continuing to remain humble and displaying good character. The way you act and handle yourself can take a person a long way. After this, Mrs. Becky stood up and read a letter to everyone. The letter was from Tourway Inn. The hotel we stayed in while we were in Florida. The letter said the following:

*Dear Mrs. Whittington,*
*I want to congratulate the Crestwood Colts on their victory (an impressive victory), and I want to thank you all for choosing Tourway Inn as your headquarters while you were in Panama City Beach. It has been a long time since I had a group in that I enjoyed as much as you all. The young men and ladies were a joy! They were polite and well mannered at all times, and no one was destructive. It is a good reflection on the young ones, but it is even more of a reflection on the excellent job the parents are doing. More power to you all.*

*Sincerely,*
*Phillip Mitchell*
*General Manager*

I think this made coach more proud of us than winning the football game. He wore a nice smile after hearing this letter.

This 85 lb team was special and had to be one of the best youth football seasons ever. We were now 30-0 after two seasons and 17-0 this year. Despite A G Gaston quitting on us in that scrimmage game, Coach placed it on our plaque as a tie. He jokingly said we were 29-0-1. Regardless of how they looked at the score, it was 8-8; even though we knew what the final score would have been. I have to give credit to our coaching staff. They were awesome and taught us so much during the season. Coach Tim led our offense to score 585 points. That equates to 34 points per game. Some of those games could have been much more, but Coach Daryl did not like to run the score up on anyone. Plus our second and third string played a lot. And what can I say about Coach Love's defense that gave up 32 points total in 17 games? A whopping 1.9 points per game average. That's less than a safety per contest. Out of those 17 games, we held our opponents scoreless in 13 of them. There were three games that we gave up one score and only one game with two scores. The two score game was in week five. After giving up six points in week 10, we never gave up another score in our last seven games. Those contests included a regular season matchup, the playoff run, and finals in Birmingham, the run through the Panama City Tourney and Finals. Averaging 34.4 points per game and giving up only 1.9 points per game.

The Crestwood 1985 - 85 lb team was amazing. The team was making its case to be the greatest youth football team of all time.

**This is my plague from the 1985 A.Y.F.L. Championship Season**

## Chapter 4
## The 100 lb

After two excellent undefeated football seasons, Coach Daryl wasted no time getting us back together. In December 1985, we got the call to play basketball. Most of the skilled and athletic players signed up. There were a couple of players who weren't quite cut out for basketball who came out, but they were primarily there to cheer us on. The games were played at St Barnabas and Saint Francis. Despite being football players, we actually had a decent basketball team that included guys such as myself, Chubb, James, Quantell, Reg, To-Jo, Terrail, Cam, and Randy. We only lost two games during the season, made the playoffs but lost in the semifinals round. Basketball presented itself as just another opportunity for us to bond closer as a family.

After basketball, the spring of 1986 rolled around, and we continued to be together as a team. Coach signed us back up for baseball. This time we played in the Bryan Weiner League; a league through the Boys and Girls Club in downtown Birmingham. We had lots of fun because many of our classmates from school were on the opposing teams. Again we fared very well in the league, and we were very competitive. During the baseball season, the other kids were still taking shots at us for our wins as a football team. As you can see, Coach invested a lot of time in us. I mean it seemed as if some of us were together year round. We literally went from football to basketball, to baseball. We got knocked out of the playoffs again in the second round to end the baseball season.

During the summer we got back together to take a team trip. The whole 85 lb team attended. The summer trip was a stroll down Hwy 20 East to Six Flags Park in Atlanta,

Georgia. The Big Green Machine was back at it again. We left Crestwood Park rolling out to Atlanta for a day of fun and games. Coach gave us direction to travel in at least a group of fours while in the park. We were to all meet back at the bus at a certain time for lunch. We rode rides, enjoyed one another and continued to build team camaraderie. These trips weren't about the offense, defense, blue, red or green jerseys or any type of competition. They were for bonding, having fun, and lots of great team experiences.

We returned from a great trip to discover some awful, disgusting news. While we were gone, someone came to our park and set the equipment room, and concession stands on fire. All of our helmets, shoulder pads, and additional equipment inside was destroyed. It felt like someone had ripped your heart right out of your chest. How could anyone do this to us? How could someone do this to coach? Who in the hell would do something like this! We were all hurt and angry at the same time. As soon as things were going great for us, here comes a disaster. I wonder if it was someone upset or jealous of our back to back undefeated seasons. Maybe they were trying to harm us and keep us from playing the next year. Coach was devastated. Shortly after the fire, we had a team meeting and ultimately decided to go back out on the streets again and ask for donations from the community. The next Saturday we went back up to the Century Plaza Mall intersection for another fundraiser. Coach informed us that whenever bad things or storms come your way, especially those out of your control, this is how you handle them. "It's ok to be sad or down, however, don't stay down forever. Eventually, you have to get up, get out, and get back to work." So that's exactly what we did. The community of Crestwood was amazing. We had a wonderful turnout, and people came out to the park to donate, as well. There was some who came from all parts of Birmingham to help out. Surrounding companies and organizations also chipped.in. Just in a short time with all of the support we received, the park was able to rebuild the concession stand and get back just about everything we had lost. Helping one another is so important to humankind, and I wish that we all can adopt that type of spirit. You never know if and when you will need someone to help you.

July came around quick, and now it was time to start practice for the next season. The league officials decided to increase all of the team's up by five pounds. So the old 65 lb went to 70 lb, 75 lb to 80 lb, 85 lb to 90 lb, 95 lb to 100 lb, 105 lb to 110 lb, and 115 lb to 120 lb. So instead of being the 95 lb, we were now the 100 lb. Changing the pounds helped us out with the players that were going to struggle to make the official weight at 95 lbs anyway. We had a couple of key players that were not returning for the 100 lb season including: linebackers Dwayne Tolbert, Quincy Weaver, and safety Preston Pratt. However, we did pick up some players after the viscous tryouts. Those players were Matthew Rodgers, Lamont Johnson, Teddy Sergeant, Marcus Peterson, Dennis Mason, Daktari Newberry, Mike Lavender, Anterio Rich, Leo Cooper, and Joe Jenkins. Along with these players, we added a couple of coaches to help out. Mathew's dad Jeremy Rodgers, Jeff's dad Bill Wildermuth helped coach the offense.

The 100 lb team was set and we were ready to start our journey to defend the title. The red and blue jersey battle was back on again. We were competing every day for all positions. No one was given a position: you had to earn your spot every year. There were also battles for second-string positions. I can't emphasize enough how hard, tough, and grimy our practices were. Monday through Friday was a grind, but Saturday was lots of fun. You got tired of beating each other up during the week, so Saturdays we had a chance to release the pain to someone else. After weeks of practice, we got our first test with a scrimmage game against a team name Vestavia. We took the Green Machine out to Vestavia, AL, (on the outskirts of Birmingham) to play them. Upon arriving, we could see their players from the bus. Their entire team was huge. After getting off the bus I just so happen to hear the conversation between their coach and ours. After seeing the size difference, Vestavia's coach asked, " Coach Daryl, you sure that you all want to play us with our size and weight difference?" Coach looked at us, then looked back at their coach and said, "Ah hell, they will be alright. " We didn't know it, but their league was different than ours, and they were a 115 lb team. They were also older than us. The game starts, and we came out hitting and aggressive. The offense was dominant and clicking on all cylinders. I don't think they were used to our team speed and toughness. We went to work and won the game 38-0. Vestavia's coach was left in awe of the play and discipline we displayed against their large team. I think coach scheduled that game knowing we would face bigger teams in the future. See, our team was fairly small overall. We had a few players that were close to 100 lbs, but not many. Next coach scheduled a game against another Metro League team by the name of East Lake Cowboys. They had a great program and had team colors of blue and red. We also knew a lot of their guys from their team because we went to school with them. Many of us from Kingston, The Shep, Avondale, and Gate City had friends playing for East Lake. They wanted us, and we wanted them. The talk of this game had been brewing for two years. East Lake knew we had whooped on Ensley and A. G. Gaston

Birmingham, but they claimed that they were the best team in the Metro League.  All week before school, they were talking trash that there was absolutely no way we could beat them.  In addition to all their bragging, East Lake Cowboys had won their championship the prior year.  So game day arrives, and we took the Green Machine up 1st Ave North to their place.  Our park was only minutes away from theirs. We are chanting all the way there followed by our fans and parents.  Man, when we got there it was so crowded we could barely get to the field.  Police officers were escorting us through the crowd.  People were everywhere, and all kinds of bets were made in the stands. We were called names and being yelled at by people saying that we were about to get our a**es kicked.  On the first drive, To-Jo hit their star tailback, Rico, so hard that he took a couple of steps backwards before falling down.  I think their fans knew we meant business right after that. We stopped them, so they had to punt the ball away.  Our first possession with the ball led to a fight.  We were running the ball down their throats when T J blocked one of their defensive lineman about 30 yards down the field, then drove him into the dirt. Nothing illegal because the whistle had not been blown.  Their players and fans got upset and tried to fight us. After the police calmed the scene down, we finished taking care of business.  Their team had a lot of athletes, and they probably intimidated others. The Colts were not going to be scared of anyone, plus we were mostly from the hood too, so we were not, at all, intimidated. Our team was well coached, smart, extremely fast, and very disciplined. Too much for the Metro League Champs on their field, we won the game 34-6.  On the way to the bus, we still heard things like you all are sorry and not that good.  I guess we were good enough that day.  Our fans were chanting. "Who dat talkin'

'bout beating them Colts, Who dat, who dat, say what?"
The win over the Eastlake Cowboys was great and lead us
into the regular season.

Trussville was our opponent for our opening game. Our
fan base had grown larger: green and white packed out the
park.  We are all on the bus chanting Colts get ready to roll,
Colts get ready to roll. (clap, ,clap, clap ). Everyone on the
team made the game weigh-in. We came down the hill in
numerical order; James stopped to eat his burger before
entering the gate. The third season for Coach Daryls  Colts
is here, baby. The announcer called us out from the goal
post in numerical order. We make the left on the 50-yard-
line, as we make our way to the sideline.  Trussville played
extremely hard and had a lot of pride. Unfortunately for
them, they were not good enough to beat us. We won the
game opener 44-6.

Our second game against Huffman was interesting.
Our team was in full stride and looking unbeatable again.
Huffman had a great crowd and was full of energy. The
game was closer than the score showed because they
played well. The Colts rolled out another win, 30-0.

Coach Daryl was still picking us up and dropping us off
to and from practice daily.  The guys in the neighborhood
who once questioned why this man was in our hood,
began to love what he was doing with us. They would
always stop and speak to him and ask how he was doing,
and they would ask if he needed anything.  See Coach had
become one of the homeboys to them. They accepted him
in the hood and looked out for him.

So we completed another week of practice and headed
over to Coach's house the next Friday to spend the night.
All of the heavyweights, the players on the route, along
with a few other who wanted to come was there.  Mrs.
Becky cooked lots of great food as usual. This particular

night we were playing and using Wilson's boxing gloves. We were always competing at something. The boxing matches were supposed to have been outside. Well, let's just say we had some squaring off inside the house. So T.J. And Chubb went at it, which resulted in bodies going through the living room window. Man, man, man, we were all sitting around nervous and scared. We knew that this was wrong; we did not follow directions and box outside. To add to the tragedy, Coach had left but was on his way back home. You could hear a pin drop in the room. We all were thinking, what will Coach say when he gets home? What will he do to us? No more spending the night for us. I just knew someone was about to be cursed out. So Coach comes into the house. I think he sensed our regretfulness, as we told him what happened. Coach forgave us for our wrongdoing without any repercussions. We had to help patch the window up tho; Coach had the window fixed the next day. Can you imagine having some kids that are not yours knocking out your living room window? Coach could have blown a gasket when he got home; however, he showed compassion and told us not to do it again. I know if we had missed a tackle or jumped offsides, he would have been all on our tails. Whew! We dodged a bullet that time.

Saturday morning, we were up and prepared for our game against Adamsville; another tough team that was well coached and talented. As usual, the defense pitched another shutout. On offense, T.J. ran for a score, and Andy ran for two. Two-point conversions were run by Mike and Chubb and a pass from James to Cam. The final score was 24-0. The next week we had a bye, but still practiced a couple of days to stay sharp. Coach had a special treat prepared for us on that bye Saturday. We were going to Legion Field to see Alabama play Notre Dame. The excitement was over the top for us to see a college game in person. Never will we forget the hit that Alabama's Cornelius Bennett put on Notre Dame's quarterback. We all went nuts after seeing that lick. Another great team experience and Alabama won the game 28-10.

After the Alabama vs Notre Dame game, we headed into the second half of the season. Tarrant would be the next opponent on the menu. Remember this was the team that had bad blood with us from all the trash talking the prior season. They came in with the same mentality this year. Close but no cigar for the Wildcats. We rolled on this Tarrant team 28-8. Our next game was against Pinson. We jumped out on them early and never looked back. Lots of guys played in this one with the final score being 72-0. The final two games of the regular season was another win against Fultondale 26-0 and the final game, another win against Leeds 48-6. The last game solidified us as National Conference Champs by winning on our side of the league.

Before the playoffs started, at practice, Coach set up scrimmages with our 110 lb team. They were a good team and had also made the playoffs. We hung in there with them without keeping the score. The scrimmage was very competitive and tough. They did have a fullback, #83, that was remarkable. #83 would be my best friend, Lorenzo. They ran a wishbone offense. Ford was big, fast and strong. He was getting 6 to 7 yards a carry, sometimes off dive plays. We had to gang tackle him at all times.

A couple of days later, Coach set up another scrimmage at the park for us. He didn't tell us who we were going against, so we assumed that it was another battle with our 110 lb team. We started walking toward their practice area, but Coach who was leading the way, passed by them. It appeared he was walking toward our

120 lb team. Coach had to be out of his mind. Yep, that's right we strolled down to scrimmage our 120 lb team. Now, I will remind you that these guys are 12, 13, and 14 years old. Our team ages are 9, 10, and 11. I weighed about 85 lbs at the time, and we were about to play some giants. Not only were our 120 lb team huge, but they were very good. See they had won the AYFL the previous year as the 110 lb and like us, were undefeated. They were led by a great coach, Coach Mark. My older cousin Marcus McKinney was on this team, along with players such as Gantry Powell, Lyndell Robinson, Terrance Byrd, Derrick Walker, Nick Boler, Thomas (June) Clark, and their quarterback Isaac (Stank) Davis. They were only a few of many talented guys on this team. Man, these guys were huge, fast, and vicious. To say we were a little intimidated was an understatement. Their offense was the best in the league, scoring 30 to 40 points per game. So we strap up and start the scrimmage. Our offense goes out first, but we could barely move the ball. Their defense was just too big and strong. We made a few good runs but just couldn't match up with them. Next, the defense went out there against them. These guys had a backfield loaded with talent behind a great offensive line. On the first drive, we stopped them from getting a first down. I think they were trying to take it easy on us. Following our stop, Coach Mark chewed their offense out; and they went full speed after that. They started to push us around at will. Man, I believe Chubb and I made most of the tackles 10 yards down the field playing safety. Coach Love had us trying our best. We filled the holes with everything we had, trying to tackle them. We didn't shy away at all, but they were still dragging us. After they beat us up, I think Coach Mark and our 120 lb team gained a whole new level of respect for Coach Daryl's Colts. We talked afterward, and they all

said they understood why we were undefeated. The 120 lb team said we came at them without hesitating and were flying all over the field in droves trying to stop them. Coach Love taught us very well how to make tackles. Coach Daryl knew that his team had plenty of guts just to put forth a valiant effort against our great 120 lb team.

The next day Coach received a phone call from Avondale School, where some our players attended. Reg, To-Jo, and Cam apparently had been acting up and not getting their lesson in school. Coach Daryl went up there and got all three players out of class, chewed them out, and whipped their butts, at school. He told them that school was important and they all were going to do better, or they will not be playing any football. Now, these were our starting wingback, receiver and middle linebacker, and offensive tackle and defensive end. There are some kids today who need that type of discipline when they act up, however in our current society everyone would be calling the cops or trying to fight or shoot the disciplinarian. After the whooping, the player's teacher saw Coach in the office crying. She stopped and asked him what was wrong? Coach trying to hold back his tears told her that he loved his boys and didn't want them to misbehave. He told her that all he wanted was for them to be successful. Coach decided to *Go For Two* and pay for the guys a tutor to help with their grades. He took care of the conduct part himself. Our assistant coach, Tim, agreed to pick them up from school, take them to the tutor, and then bring them to practice. If the tutor gave any bad reports, they would not be allowed to practice. See Coach Daryl always put education before football, and he meant it. He explained to the guys that they might not be "A" students, but they were going to give an "A" effort. He told them that there was no excuse not to act right in the classroom. He told their teacher to call him if she had any more problems out of them. Reg told me that they were so far behind that he's not sure how they caught up and passed that year. The compassion coach showed for them at the school that day, along with the extra tutor help allowed their teacher to pass them. From Reg, ToJo, and Cam. Thanks, Coach.

The Friday before the playoffs started, we ended practice early, and all headed to a Halloween costume party in Downtown Birmingham: a fun treat for us to get out and fellowship with the guys. The Halloween party was held annually for the kids and adults to come out and have fun. After that we left and went to the haunted house on the Southside of Birmingham. These big, bad, undefeated football players (speaking of us all) were piled up in every corner we turned down, scared to see what was next. Lots of pushing and shoving went on, along with laughter and fun.

The first round of the playoffs was the next day, and we played Pinson at home. We were ready to defend our title and go for the three-peat. We had just beat Pinson a couple of weeks prior by a score of 42-0. They came out fast on their first drive and took advantage of a busted coverage to go up 8-0. On our first drive, we fumbled the ball and gave them the ball in excellent field position. They scored again and went up 14-0 right out the gate. Their fans were all going crazy. We were all shell-shocked. Meanwhile, Coach Darryl is letting us have it. I'm not sure if it was the late night at the haunted house, but we had to get our act together and soon, or our winning streak would be over. Our sideline was not the place to be after being down 14-0. This game against Pinson was the first time we had been down by two scores in three years. All of our pounds, including the 110 lb team and the120 lb team was cheering us on. The cheerleaders, fans, and Mom Squad were looking puzzled, but still rooting for us. Man, it was like a bolt of lightning hit us hard and fast. We took our next drive and ran the ball down their throats to score, and that was all she wrote. The defense finally got it together and held them to just those 14 points. The offense went wild and scored every time they touched the ball. The score ended up being 50-14 at halftime. Yes. Halftime. We went to our sidelines and looked on the other sideline, and they were taking off their helmets and shoulder pads. They left the field at the half and never looked back.

The semi-finals came, and the game would be against Center Point. We were one game away from making it to our third straight championship game appearance. Center Point was extremely talented and had a very physical group. They played us tooth and nail but they ended up falling short by a score of 26-0. The championship game was next on the agenda. We were all ecstatic to be going back to the finals.

This particular year the finals were to be held at Hewitt Trussville High School, instead of the usual spot at Lawson Field. Our opponent this time was South Roebuck. They were hot and playing great ball, led by their star quarterback, Benjamin. South Roebuck threw the ball all around the yard. Playing safety, I knew I would love this type of game. However, I had an issue come up that was not going to be good for me. We had just received our report cards, and I had gotten a D in conduct. My mom was livid and told me that I couldn't play the upcoming game on Saturday. I'm like, "Ma, this is the championship game." Mom insisted, "It don't matter, you can't play." I tried to explain what happened, but had no luck changing my mom's mind. Not playing in the championship game was the punishment I had to take for being guilty by association. See there were some guys in my class cracking jokes about our teacher. Unfortunately, these guys were sitting right behind me in the class. The teacher gave those guys an F in conduct, and everyone around them who laughed a D in conduct. I have to admit, the joke was funny, and I was laughing, but that was about it. Anyone that knows me, knows that I'm silly and that joke was hilarious. Still, to this day, I don't believe that one laughing incident in six weeks shouldn't have gotten me a D in conduct. Coach even tried to convince my mom to let me play because he had never had any issues with me before. No dice from my mom, however, she allowed me to go and watch. Watching on the sidelines was worst than not playing. Watching South Roebuck throw the ball almost every down was hard to see; especially, when their quarterback hit Roderick Toyer for a 36-yard touchdown. Also, he hit Anthony Hammond on an 86-yard bomb. Those were the only scores they had, but it was not going to be enough; we went up, scoring 50. Cam scored on a 20-yard pass from James and Cam scored on a 13-yard reverse. Randy had two touchdowns runs of 18 and 22 yards. Andy scored once, and Chubb ran an interception back for a 35-yard score. Charley added a 3-yard run and Mike, and Andy added some two-point conversions. The final score: 50-12. Celebration again! Our fans went nuts. Here we are; the three-time undefeated AYFL champs. This was a great time to be a Colt. Who dat talkin bout beating them Colts, who dat, who dat , say what. After all of the celebrations, Coach advised us that we had been chosen to play in the Alabama State Youth Football Invitation. This was not just one of the local individual leagues, but it represented the entire state of Alabama. The state invited only four teams to play which ultimately continued our season again.

Thompson was one of the four teams invited. They were representing as champs from the Jefferson County League. A. G. Gaston Bessemer, the Metro League Champs, was also invited. Finally, Central Park, who was a one lost playoff team in our league. We didn't get to play Central Park during our season because they lost in the playoffs before the finals. So their fans were itching to play us. They would get their wish because that's who we drew in the semifinal. And Thompson squared off against A.G Gaston Bessemer. We played first and rolled over Central Park 50-6 to move on to the State Finals. We watched the next matchup in which both teams played hard, but Thompson won the game. So the State finals were set. Crestwood vs. Thompson. Both teams were good, and both fan bases were excited to play. The State semifinals and championship games were held at North Highland Park in Hueytown, AL. We arrived on the Green Machine for the finals. The park was packed, and there was not an empty seat anywhere. The game is physical, and we went back and forth the first half with each team not scoring. We came out the second half and gained momentum by scoring twice. We lead 12-0 at the end of the 3rd quarter as we started a drive led by Mike who ran for 30 yards on four carries. We chanted our famous 4th quarter chant from the field to the sidelines: *4th quarter, our quarter, 4th quarter, our quarter*. We started the final quarter with a reverse, faking it to Mike and giving it to Randy who would score from 28 yards out. We wore them down in the end to take a commanding 30-0 lead, with 4:58 remaining, Thompson would finally get on the scoreboard. Their receiver Phillip Busby caught a pass that I tipped for a score. I was playing the left side safety in a cover two defense, but saw the receiver open on the opposite sidelines. Our right safety came up and left the receiver by himself. When I saw this, I tried to go over and cover my teammate. Unfortunately, I dove and only got a hand on the ball which he caught off the tip and scored. Despite my efforts to back my teammate's area, Coach Daryl and my teammates had to joke about it. They were saying things like, "Corey, I smell burnt toast." Now here I am trying to cover my partner, and I'm catching the heat. I guess they had to get me back because I was always talking trash about being the best cover guy. We would come back and score again, late with an 8-yard run from Randy. Chubb ran in the two-point conversion to make the final score 38-6. Verdell, Reg, Jeremy, Edmund, and Jesse led the defense. So here we are the third year in a row, undefeated National Conference Champs, third-year AYFL Champs, and the Alabama State Champs. What a year in football for the Coach Daryl 100lb Crestwood Colts.

The following week, Coach took us on a camping trip to Mt. Cheaha State Park. This park has the highest point in Alabama at 2407 feet above sea level. The state park is located at the top of Cheaha Mountain. The camping areas are at the top of the mountain. I'll never forget the day we left Crestwood Park going on another new adventure: this would be my, and several others, first camping trip. It was a mild sunny afternoon, probably around 65 to 70 degrees. My mom brought me a heavy jacket, in which I didn't want to take because I didn't want to carry it; and it was warm outside anyway. So I told my mom that I didn't need it and I'll just take the smaller jacket. I will be fine with only the smaller one. Please listen to your parents! So we left Crestwood Park migrating to the campsite. After arriving, we stepped off the bus, and looked around at the scenery in amazement. Shortly after getting settled, we walked back down to the store that we spotted on our way up the mountain. We went into to the store, and the weather was beautiful. Everyone was getting snacks and drinks while inside. The strangest thing happened, it started to drizzle; however, no one had an umbrella.  So we take off running back up the hill. Before we can get far, the rain was turning into snow.  Ah man, I should have gotten that dang jacket my mom tried to get me to take.  The weather took a nosedive, and it was cold the rest of the trip.  There were about thirty of us players on the first day. We had lots of fun, played and went on hiking trails. The first night we slept in sleeping bags inside the tents.  Everyone sat around the campfire and roasted marshmallows and hot dogs. We laughed and told jokes all night. I'll never forget when Coach told all of us that whoever came into your tent last, make sure the zipper is closed all the way down. Guys started to call it a night one at a time and retire into the tents. I started to get sleepy and went inside my tent. I didn't realize it, but the way I was sleeping my feet was turned toward the zipper.  ToJo was the last one to come into our tent and accidentally left the zipper cracked open. The temperature continued to drop, that night and I woke up the next morning with my feet frostbitten. Oh my, my, my, I had never felt that kind of pain before. It was a strange feeling because they said it was a frostbite, but as my feet thawed, they felt like someone had a blowtorch pointed at them.  The mornings, in general, were crazy, because you had to walk down a little ways to the cold showers. The only person who got warm water was Jeremy. He would get up around four or five in the morning to go shower.  After that, the water was freezing cold. Those were probably the fastest showers taken in history.  It had gotten so cold outside that we were around the campfire during the daytime trying to stay warm. One afternoon the guys were playing around the campfire and ToJo's pants caught on fire.  We didn't know what to do. He was panicking and we were panicking too. All of a sudden Coach Daryl came running toward us at full speed. For three years Coach had been teaching us how to tackle, and we finally saw him in action. Coach had good form and technique, too, as he tackled ToJo and rolled him in the dirt and grass to put the fire out. Coach Daryl saved the day and cautioned us about the danger of horseplaying around the campfire. Each day guys were leaving because of the cold weather. Coach had to turn on the generator on the bus for us to stay warm. We made sleeping pallets across the seats of the bus at night due to the outside temperature. We played cards and watched movies as well. We must have watched the movie LaBamba about 20 times. It was a great movie. All I can think about is the word "Richieeeee." If you saw the movie, you know exactly what part that was. The last day before returning home, a couple of guys went on another hiking trail. Would you believe that they got lost? It was only about a couple of miles; then they were to return. After so long, we knew that they were lost. Coach grabbed his compass and headed out looking for them. A couple of hours passed and we are all getting nervous. But out of nowhere we saw that cowboy hat. It was Coach returning with the guys that went out. We sat around the campfire that night hearing all kinds of noises in the woods. We laughed and cracked jokes about all of the things that went on during the trip. As stated earlier, a lot of the parents came and picked up their kids each day because of the harsh weather. There were only 15 players, returning on the Green Machine, who were able to handle the tough, yet fun outing.

A couple of weeks later we had our annual banquet. This one would be very special. Despite so many things that took place that year, there was one more surprise. Coach received some help to fulfill one of our wishes. The previous year the 1985 Chicago Bears won the Super Bowl and ultimately did a rap video called the Super Bowl Shuffle. For my younger generation, Google the Super Bowl Shuffle to see it. We thought the bears were great, especially the defense. Just like the Colts 100 lb team. We asked Coach if we won the championship, could we do a rap video like the Bears. So for weeks, we practice the rap song, and it was hilarious doing the sessions. We could play some football, but everyone could not rap. We messed up in rehearsal over and over again. Finally, we got it right and performed it at the banquet. We had on our jerseys with a pair of blue jeans, and we're ready to give our parents and fans a treat. The song was written by James Bevels Jr, Quinton Evans, Marvin Jones, and Andrea Woodley.

The 1986 100lb Crestwood Colts Shuffle went a little something like this.

Mike:   *Me Cam and Andy, we run the ball*
         *our offensive line is doing they all*

Chubb: *they call me hoss and I get respect*
         *to run touchdowns is what I expect*

Mike: *we got Reg and Leo at offensive tackle*
         *their giving the defense a whole of lot of hassle*

Indiv:  *Quontell, Demetrius, Mauricus, and Dennis*
         *To the whole defense- we spell menace*
         *Cause Joe does swell and  Randy runs well*
         *Off tackle, they run behind me Verdell*
         *We the two bad ends and there are no others*
         *I'm Terrail - I'm ToJo - we the Saffo brothers*

*To lead the O- we've got the knack*
*Willie, Matt, James we play quarterback*
*We shock the crowd like a thunderbolt*
*Scoring all the points for the Crestwood Colts*

*DEFENSE.DEFENSE.DEFENSE DEFENSE*

*We're always hard never ever soft*
*So listen up good as the backs count off*
*I'm Charley- I'm Corey - I'm Cam- I'm Hoss*
*We the def backs- we don't quit- we never lost*
*We scare the offense with a small grunt*
*I'm Marcus- This is Jeff- and this is Munt*
*We're linebackers, but they're more u see*
*There's Andy, Charles, Mike and even Willie*
*The defensive line is the sack attack*
*We kill the runners and the quarterbacks*
*James, Jeremy, Jesse, T. J.*
*The defensive line is the position we play.*
*Big Dog and Reg u know we did it*
*Playing defensive end line Cornelius Bennett*
*Stopping the run and setting new trends*
*Corey, Teddy,& Lamont are the defensive ends*
*Crestwood is sure to have the clout*
*When our defense shuts the other team out*
*We song this song with the gang all here*
*We hope to win it again next year*
*45-0 is all great and good*
*Let's hear it for the Colts of Crestwood*

Yep, we turned it out with that jam! The crowd gave us a standing ovation. The banquet was a great and memorable night. To make things even more special, we received a few letters from some notable persons about our accomplishments. Coach Daryl got up and read them to us. Here is the first letter:

*"Dear Crestwood Colts -*
*I am happy to join others who have gathered to salute you. The 100 lb Crestwood Colts. You are winners of the sort that we can all be proud of. I commend you for your sparkling play on the field and for your exceptional display of character of people. Your record of not having tasted the sting of defeat for three years is an inspiration to us all. Your deeds on the athletic field hopefully are but a prelude to future achievements in life later on. While I am at it, permit me to congratulate your parents and your coaches who have guided your lives, enabling you to arrive at such a lofty place of honor. Congratulations, and may God bless you all.*
*Sincerely, Mayor Richard Arrington Jr.*
*November 1986. "*

The second letter read:
*"To the Crestwood Colts Football Team.*
*Congratulations to all of you for your outstanding season. Having been involved in athletics as a player and as a coach most often in life; I know the hard work, sacrifices, dedication, and effort it takes to be successful. Your athletic careers are just beginning, and I want to wish you all the best as you continue to grow in wisdom, knowledge, and athletic ability. Winning and losing is certainly important, that's the reason we keep score. Let us never forget that athletics make men strong; study makes men wise; character makes men great. My very best wishes to each of you for continuing success and War Eagle.*
*Sincerely, Pat Dye Athletic Director and Head Coach of Auburn University. Nov 24, 1986."*

The third letter read:

*"Dear members of the Colts football team. I would like to congratulate you on another undefeated season. This is a tremendous accomplishment, and I am personally proud of each one of you. It takes a lot of discipline, sacrifices, and hard work to achieve the goals you set in life, academically and athletically you are to be commended. Again Congratulations on a great season and best wishes to you and your coaches for continued success.*

*Sincerely, Ray Perkins- Alabama Athletic Director and Head Coach. Dec 9th, 1986."*

It was truly surprising and an honor to be recognized by the City of Birmingham's Mayor along with Alabama and Auburn University. Coach also talked to us about remaining humble in our success. Also, we heard the same speech since the 75 lb team about the football having a funny bounce to it, and at any time the ball could possibly not bounce our way. He challenged us to stay focus, work hard, and make the 110 lb team next season even better.

Now let's find out if Coach Daryl's Colts can continue to roll in Chapter 5's 110 lb.

**Crestwood Colts 100 lb Team**

## Chapter 5
## The 110 lb

After the 100 lb football season, Coach Daryl's Colts continued to roll. We went back into the basketball league at Saint Barnabas, a Catholic school and church in Birmingham. Playing basketball was helpful in improving our footwork and agility. It also kept the guys in shape until football season came back around. We won most of our regular season basketball games and did very well. The crew of about 12 players continued to spend the night over Coach's house. Sometimes before and after basketball games, and especially on the weekend. We use to play in the backyard, shooting hoops in Wilson's goal. This is where we met Queenie, Wilson's dog, who mostly stayed out back. She was a very nice and playful. One Saturday she got a little jealous of us and sat down right under the basket and would not move. I guess she was saying nobody can play if I can't. Quennie was also very protective of Wilson. One afternoon To-Jo and Wilson were playing around wrestling, and I guess Queenie thought To-Jo was harming Wilson. She took off and ran over and bit To Jo on the rear end. Shocking for Queenie, because she would never bite a fly. However, it was funny to us guys, and we all laughed it off, even To Jo. So back on the court we finished the regular season and headed to the playoffs. Several guys played exceptional all basketball season: Anterio, Chubb, Quon, To-Jo, Wilson, Mauricus, Randy, Terrail, Charles, Cam, and myself. We ended up beating St. Francis in the finals to take home another championship. We all had plenty of fun and enjoyed the season.

In spring of 1987, the Colts switched their uniforms, once again to the gloves, hats, and cleats to play baseball.

Most of the same guys that played baseball were on the basketball team. James and Andy were standouts on the baseball team. They both were playing on All-Star teams, so they helped us out tremendously. In one of our practice sessions, Coach Daryl stood behind the catcher calling strikes and balls. James was pitching and threw one of his speedy fastballs. It was too much for the catcher to handle and the ball hit Coach in the eye. The lick smashed his shades but luckily didn't damage his eye socket. Coach had a nasty bruise that flared up, but Coach shook it off and continued to coach. This year we played in the Irondale League in which had some excellent teams. Some of the teams had been playing together for years. Each week we got better and better. I can remember hitting my very first home run over the fence during the season. I'll never forget it was a 0-2 pitch count in which the umpire called both strikes on pitches that were down by my ankles. Chubb was in the batter's box batting behind me saying, "C'mon Corey, don't strike out man." So the next pitch came, again headed for my ankles, so I went golfing and hit one out of the park. Mauricus, (Dale Murphy) Green, should remember that one. So we continue to progress as the season went by and made it to the playoffs. This time we fell short and lost in the playoffs. The progress from our first season to now was incredible in baseball. Only bigger and better things were to come.

The summer of 1987 arrived, and the Crestwood Colts were back in business. The football tryouts were upon us. Most of the 100 lb team is back. However, we did lose a few guys like Quontell, Charley, and Matthew. We had 20-30 additional guys that came out on top of the close to 40 players already on the team. After the workouts, running and conditioning there were a few players that made it. A few notable players were Charles Che Jackson, Calvin , and Billy Latham.  Our practice was  always hard, but ever so often something funny happened. One of those moments gave a player his nickname. We were doing a drill where two players were competing with speed and pulling themselves up a rope.  Anterio was climbing up the rope trying to beat his opponent when his shorts fell down. Coach said aloud, "Man this guy has a black duke." Anterio was a dark-skinned brother who was a  good player.  All of us had to laugh including Anterio.  So that's was his name the rest of the season (Black Duke).  Coach Daryl was really pushing us this season.  Teams were getting closer to us and started filming our plays. They knew our formation. You could see it at the end of the 100 lb season. Whenever we line up with a strong side formation, the defenses would shift to that way before the snap.  Coach Daryl and Coach Tim started adding new wrinkles such as misdirection to run away from the strong side.  We started something new where the quarterbacks call the plays from the line of scrimmage.  Just like the past three years, this was something that the first, second, and third string were going to have to learn. We had been successful for three years, and this is where all the magic happened: at practice.  Coach would often quote this phrase to us. "Everybody wants to win, but everybody don't want to prepare to win." It all comes together from hard work, discipline, and practice. For three years coach signaled out plays in from the sidelines with hand signals. Now we were about to take it to another level. James and Wilson was giving the privilege to call the plays at the line of scrimmage without a huddle. This was put in place to keep defenses honest when they played us. Our base offense was two tight ends. Also a pro set backfield, meaning the fullback and tailback on each side of the quarterback. Finally the wingback would be strong left or right. Now we started practicing placing all three backs stacked behind the quarterback. There were three colors called follows by three numbers. For example, James and Wilson would survey the defense first then call out Red 22, Black 11, Blue 46. Next everyone would shift to the play. After shifting, the quarterback would say, "Team down, sed, hike." In this particular example, the color red 22 would be a dummy number. This means it has nothing to do with the play. Secondly the color black 11 is the snap count, so the play will be on the first hike. Finally, the color blue 46 is the play: pro set, wing right cross block 46. Everyone who played on offense had to learn this. The offensive line also did an excellent job because they had to listen for the play and snap count as well. On plays like the cross block 46, the right end had to block down on the defensive tackle, and the tackle had to pull and block the defensive end. We went over these hundreds of times at practice with the first, second, and third-string offense. Because we practiced the plays in this way and knew the codes, it was helpful for our offense because our opponents would not have time to adjust to us. Now keep in mind, we had lots of problems trying with this at first. Players would forget what color meant what. Some would forget the count and start jumping offsides. Sometime we went the wrong way on the play. However after many, many, many, many, reps we started to get it right. Example 2: Red 86, Black 22, Blue 33. Can you figure it out? I'll give it to you. Red 86 is nothing. The snap count is 2 (Black 22). And the play is a power 33. The backs also have to shift and line up in the correct spot for the call. All of our backs knew their called run. Anything in the 20's.

The wingback play: 24, 28 toss, etc. The tailbacks were any 30's. Power 33 and finally the fullback plays were all in the 40's, for example, Crossblock 45/46. The quarterbacks still had to make sure everyone was in their correct spots and set before starting the play. All of this was pretty impressive and took lots of practice. Let me tell you what was more impressive: the colors would change each week. So black would change from the dummy call to the snap count. Red would change from the count to the play. And blue would switch from the play to the dummy call. The colors changed to prevent our opponents from keeping up with us and cheating on our plays. I knew other teams couldn't cheat cause hell, we barely could remember what colors meant what ourselves. Coach Love also adjusted the defense some as well. We kept our famous Reddog defense. Reddog is where everyone blitzed except the two safeties. He installed a lot of different zone and blitz packages, even sending the safeties, too. Teams were throwing the ball more, now, so we played some man to man coverage: cover two, three, and four.

After weeks of practice, our first test of the 110 lb team was a practice game against West End. These guys were another team from the Metro League. We went to their field to battle. They were big, fast, and good. We made a lot of errors with the new offensive system, especially with the snap count. After a few possessions we picked it up, and things started clicking. We ran away in the second half to win the game 34-12. After the game, we came back to practice the next day and worked on our mistakes and continued to try and perfect our craft.

Before the season started, Coach Daryl took us on another trip to Cherokee Beach located in Helena, Alabama. We went the Saturday before our game and had lots of fun. We swam, ate and enjoyed each other, once again. These trips were so important because they allowed us to bond while off the field. It also allowed us to relax from all of the competition and just be boys. We returned from the beach to head into the season ready to roll. Coach purchased all of us some brand new black Nike cleats so everyone would look the same. Reginald told me that he wore his cleats to school because they looked better than his sneakers. He said that all of the kids were complimenting him and asking him where did he get those new shoes? He replied by saying, "Ah man, don't worry about that," as he flaunted them in class. The classmates never noticed that they were football cleats.

So now we get to game one, and the park is packed as usual. We're on the bus chanting and getting hype. We come down the ramp headed to the field. Before entering the field, James stops and gets his hamburger from his mom, and we're ready to roll. Our introductions were announced, one-by-one, as we file in to defend our title. The cheerleaders and Mom squad are all chanting and singing together. Sometimes you couldn't tell the difference between the two. The parents knew all of the cheers and would sing and dance with the cheerleaders. They would sing songs like "Fight the Power" and "Who Rocks the House." I know y'all remember this one: *Who rocks the house, the Colts rocks the house and when the Colts rock the house, they rock it all the way down.* The moms and cheerleaders would be down low to ground at that verse of the cheer. The next one was everyone's favorite that went like this: *Fight (clap, clap) fight the power- fight that power- fight (clap, clap) fight the power, fight the power.* Then each cheerleader would take turns saying, *"Well my name is _ and guess what imma do - I'm gonna, fight the power and (cabbage patch) too."* They would do the dance that they called out. This would always be followed by "*Oooh*" or "*Ok nigh*" from the crowd. Each cheerleader would get their turn calling out their choice of dance. Some of the moms would be dancing right along with them. I think the crowd favorite was when a cheerleader would say, *"Imma break it down on you."* Man, the stands were always loud and crunk.

Back to the field where we came out right where we left off the previous year. We knocked off Huffman 30-8 to start the season. Mike and Andy led the way on offense, while James and T.J were solid on defense. Over the next couple of weeks, we continued to grow as a unit, winning our next three games placing us at 4-0. It was at this point a funny thing started to take place. Except for our Mom Squad, cheerleaders, and fans, everywhere we went, other people wanted us to lose. The remarks that we heard while playing away was awful. It seems as if people were hoping with all their might each week that we would go down. When you are doing well and being successful people will cheer for a while, then sooner or later they will get tired of you winning, become jealous, and want you to fall from the top. Despite the backlash, we continued to fight and progress. One Sunday a teammate invited all of us to church. It was a very small church which we may have had more players on the team than they had members. It was hot with no central air. However, the people were nice to us. The singing and preaching were fantastic. We learned that all of the trips we went on, and all the success we had, none of it would be possible without God. The sermon basically was about leaning on each other and trusting God and to not put our faith in people. This was a perfect sermon for what we were dealing with.

We continued to win and finished the halfway mark of the season with a huge win over Pinson: 38-0. After that, we had a bye week, however we had been chose to play an All-Star Team from out of town. We had no information about them, except they were a team put together to beat us. Apparently, they were tired of hearing about us and wanted to do something about it. They called Coach and told him that they would come to our field and destroy us. The word traveled rapidly all over Birmingham about the game. Coach took on the challenge and accepted the matchup. We didn't even know where they were from. They showed up with around 60-70 players with decent size. A lot of other teams came to watch this game as well. From the time they arrived, we heard all kinds of trash talk and cursing, even from their coaches. As we were weighing in, all of their players, fans and coaches were degrading us. Coach Daryl simply would say, "We do our talking on the field." Do you know how hard it is to be quiet when people are calling you names for about 20 minutes straight? We loaded up on the bus and you can tell our coaches were not happy. Coach Daryl told us to do our talking with our pads. This was one of only a handful of games where Coach did stop us from scoring. So much for the All-Star team: we stomped them by a score of 73-0. After the game the All-Star team did not shake our hands. This was getting really crazy. The more we won, the more people started to hate us. So now the second half of the season starts and we are still undefeated. Practices are hard as we continued to battle for the green jerseys to wear on Friday's. Our next game was against Fultondale, and our defensive coach, Coach Love was going to be out. Coach Pratt filled in on calling the plays for this game. Man, we had to have run Reddog about 40 times. Pratt kept saying, "Man, I like that Reddog." Fultondale was not pulling off the upset this Saturday. Coach didn't like to run the score up on anyone, as we carried a 32-0 lead into the fourth quarter. Next Coach tells Wilson on the sideline to fumble the ball on purpose on the next play. He was trying to help our opponent out a little. Wilson takes the next snap, and two hand toss the ball over his head about ten yards behind him. They did recover the ball, but Coach was livid at his son. Coach screamed, "Wilson what in the hell are you doing !" Wilson responds, "You told me to fumble the ball." Coach said, "Yes, but I didn't want the whole park to know it. We all laughed at that one, but Coach was hot. The next week we played Leeds and they had gotten better and it showed. I'll never forget this game because I had an interception toward the end of the game and got hurt on the return. For some crazy reason I had flipped my knee pads inside out trying to cool off. So when I was running the interception back, my flap went up just as I was taking a hit on the knee with a helmet. So I'm lying on the ground for a while in pain. The coaches came out to check on me to see if I was alright. I roll over and guess who I see standing over me to see if I was ok. My mom. I'm like "Ma, what are you doing out here!" She responds, "Ah boy, I'm just checking on you." Then I say, "Ma, the football field is no place for moms." I was fine, just a little dinged up. We still laugh and joke about that today. Mom told me that the rest of the Mom Squad told her to check on me. She said they told her, "Cassandra, that's your boy out there hurt, you need to go see about him." Leeds fought hard, but we prevailed to win 28-14. We ended up finishing the regular season as National League Champs, once again: undefeated at 10-0 heading into the playoffs.

Back at practice we were still battling. See the only people that were slowing down our offense was our own defense. And just about the only ones who were scoring on our defense was our offense. Our scrimmages were so intense that often times the other pounds would be looking at our practice instead of their own. If they finished before us, they would come over to get a close-up view of our battles. Normally, our green jersey battles went through Thursday to determine the winner of the week. This particular week the defense had been winning the entire week. It was clear that by Thursday's practice the defense was going to win and wear the green jerseys that Friday. We were going to do less running, drink Gatorade and hold bragging rights. I think Coach Daryl knew the offense was not going to come back. However, he wanted to see their effort. I don't know if we were playing that well or the offense was just having a bad week. That's not what Coach wanted going into the playoffs. On one play during the scrimmage, Munt hit Andy so hard in the backfield. Someone missed a block, and after the lick, all you heard was Coach Love shouting, "Munty, Munty, Munty!" Love was letting the offense have it. Out of frustration, Coach Daryl yelled out to Love, "You all need to stop cheating!" Coach Love didn't take that too well, and the two coaches got into a heated argument right on the spot. Harsh words were exchanged, pushing and shoving followed. Man, we were about to have a major rumble. We didn't know what to do. All I know is we weren't cheating. There were a few times where the offensive play didn't work, and Coach Daryl would yell "Run it again, Run it again!" So obviously we knew the play, but we weren't going to let them just run over us. When I tell you this was a heated moment between two fiery competitors. Oh my God! Coach Tim and the rest of our coaches had to separate them. After they were pulled apart from one another, I'll never forget what happened next. The offense huddled up, and we huddled back up as well. Coach Love had us in the huddle so tight, I think he could have knocked all 11 of us down with one swing. He was still pissed off, breathing hard with his fists balled up. The look in his eyes was full of rage. Hell, we were all scared. He told us to listen up and listen up well dammit. He said don't you EVA (yes, I said EVA) apologize to anyone in your life for kicking their ass! Love said that you always work hard, prepare, be disciplined and play relentless at all times. He told us to never take a back seat to anyone. He yelled, "Do y'all hear me?" We replied, "Yes Sir!" At this same time, I heard the offense screaming, "Yes Sir!" as well. I don't know what Coach Daryl was saying to the offense, but I can imagine that it was a fiery speech also. So after the fiasco, we started to continue the scrimmage. The offense calls their play and breaks the huddle. Coach Love grabbed us, looked us in the eyes and called the defense, Reddog. Reddog, ready, break! Again this is where we sent nine players on the blitz. He looked at Chubb and I who were the two safeties that were not blitzing and said, "I want y'all two to blitz also." Love sent all 11 defenders at the offense: this was the first play after the fight. Needless to say, we stopped them in the backfield again. After that play, Coach Daryl called practice for the day. I guess you can say we earned those green jerseys to wear that Friday. At the end of practice Coach Daryl got the whole team together, as we all huddle up taking a knee. Both Coach Daryl and Coach Love hugged and apologized to us for the way they handled that situation. They told us that they got caught up in the competition and lost their cool. This was great and made us feel better because the offense and defense were literally split, almost feeling like two different teams. The whole situation showed us that we all make mistakes, but real men admit their faults, apologize, and continue to move forward. What a valuable life lesson we learned on that Thursday night.

The next day after practice we headed to Coach's house to spend the night. We're all in the living room watching film and getting ready for the playoffs. Now, keep in mind that there are nearly thirty guys in there all eating and playing. Everything was going smoothly until we heard a funny noise. We really couldn't tell what it was, but it sounded like some chains rattling. Coach had three boxers that were downstairs. They were not allowed upstairs, especially with all of us being there. The dogs had to have heard all of the noise upstairs and wanted to see what was going on. They used their heads to pry the door open from downstairs and ran up the steps and then opened the door that led to the kitchen. The three huge boxers made their way into the house to join the party. Can you say TOTAL PANDEMONIUM! Y'all, when they ran in that living room, we went berzerk. The huge heads of those dogs were amazing. Players were jumping on couches, running upstairs, furniture and lamps were falling on the floor. Some guys were trying to run outside. The dogs were feeding off our energy, and running wild. One of the dogs followed us upstairs. Players were jumping on the beds with their sneakers on. It was a mess. Wilson was trying to tell us to stop running and the boxers would stop, but I don't think nobody was listening to that. Wilson was doing his best, trying to calm us down. He was catching falling furniture and trying to grab the dogs. I don't know how he got all three, but I think Amy and Amanda each grabbed one of the dogs. All I know is I was not looking back to find out. I guess the dogs thought we were playing and having fun, but what they didn't realize was we were running for our lives. The dogs didn't hurt anyone; they were just playing and enjoying all of the action. Another fun-filled, crazy night at the Whittington's house. They had to have wanted to kick all of us out that night.

The next morning we started the playoffs to defend our title and possibly make it four in a row. The opponent was going to be Huffman. This team had really progressed over the season and was playing great football. Their fans were confident, and so were ours. They led 8-6 after the first quarter. Every game toward the end got closer and closer. People were starting to smell our first lost as a team. It seemed like everyone in the AYFL, and the surrounding leagues were waiting for us to go down. They would have to wait another week because we rallied to win 24-14 to move to the semifinals. Another victory over a great team and close game for the Colts.

We moved on to play Center Point in the semifinal round. We played another tight game and another great opponent. This game was 0-0 at the end of the third quarter. Both teams played very well and were looking to make it to the finals. Andy broke the scoreless game in the fourth quarter with a remarkable touchdown run. The defense was again spectacular keeping their powerful offense out of the end zone. Mike scored on a 20-yard run to ice the game at 14-0. Can you believe it? The Colts were going to its fourth straight championship. This time we found out that the opponent would be Central Park. This team had been chipping at us since we were on the 75 lb team, and they were ready to take us down.

However before we can get to the finals, we went back out on the town for ice cream. This was to celebrate making it to the finals again. Coach took us on the Green Machine for a little outing. We were hanging out at 5 Points South, an entertainment district in Birmingham with eating places and people that came there to hang out. We were parked sitting on the bus eating our ice cream being kids; the guys were talking out of the windows and speaking to people passing by. This guy who had his hair colored orange, and cut into a Mohawk with spikes in them came up to the bus. I guess he had the whole punk rock thing going on. He had to have been drunk because he was cursing and yelling at us. Coach Daryl who was in the driver seat heard the guy and was watching out for us. This dude was calling us names and saying what he was going to do to us. Someone on the bus yelled, "Man, we not scared of you." This guy loses it, snaps open a big knife and makes a B Line for the entry of the bus. He actually runs a step or two on the bus cursing with the knife in his hand. Coach Daryl pulled out the 38 pistol from underneath the seat, pointed it at the guy and said, "If you touch one of my boys, your ass won't make it off this bus." Dude quickly changed his mind, put the knife away, and ran away. We never saw that guy again. Coach Daryl was being the protector that night and once again saves the day.

Crestwood versus Central Park was the lineup for the finals. The field was packed, and we were ready to roll. From the start of the game, we went back and forth. Both teams were playing great defense. No one scored in the first quarter, and both teams and fans were a little nervous. Despite the nerves, both sidelines were cheering out of their minds. At halftime, there is still no score. Could the dynasty be over? Is this the game Coach kept talking about where the ball won't bounce our way? The second half started but seemed like every time a team got into scoring position, something happened. We finally get on the board when Wilson hit Cam on a pass to go up 6-0. This is where the score stayed at the end of the third quarter. Central Park strikes to start the fourth quarter to make the game 6-6. We would answer when Andy scored on a run to put us up 12-6. The Colts nation went wild. Central Park came right back and is driving, but the Colts threw an interception to stall their drive. Terrail catches a score from James to put us up for good to win 18-6. This was a great effort from Central Park. Nevertheless, the

Crestwood Colts 110 lb team are the AYFL Champs. Four years in a row and undefeated. The bottles are out again with the celebration. The Mom Squad was yelling, *We are proud of you, and We are proud of you!*." Despite our joy, there was still a lot of people upset that we won another one. We were chanting, Who dat talkin bout beating them colts, who dat, who dat, say what. What a year, what a team, I can't believe we did it again. Everyone is proud that the mission was accomplished after all of the hard work. There we were again, Coach Daryl's 110lb Crestwood Colts being as bad as we wanna be. However, after the season we ran upon some guys who were a lot "badder" than us.

We took another trip on the Green Machine to face our toughest foe, yet. This would be a ride down to West Jefferson Prison. Coach always talked to us about life, and about the decisions we made on a daily basis. He warned us that if we don't work hard, don't have self-discipline, don't listen to our parents, and decide to do bad things, that there is a place for those types of people. That place is where he took us so that we could see for ourselves. The day we walked in and they slammed that huge steel door behind us, you knew that this was the real deal. They gave us a tour of the cells which they slept on those hard surfaces with a thin mat on top of it. They told us about the limited supplies that you are allowed such as soap and tissue. We walked to an area where about 30 inmates, sitting on bleachers, watched a small T.V. We also saw the shower area, which was an open glass so that anyone could see in. Man, I knew this was not the place I wanted to come back to, especially not to stay. They showed us how weapons had been formed from melted down lotion bottles on a piece of metal to make a knife. Finally, some of the guys sat down with us and shared their personal stories. Some of the guys who were from outside of the prison and some who were from inside the prison. They talked to us about our decisions and watching the crowd of people we hung around. They said a lot of people were inside from just being with the wrong crew. Some who thought they had friends and in reality, they didn't. I remember one guy told us, "If they get you into trouble, then that's not your friend." This was an eye-opener and a great lesson learned by all of us on the team.

We returned from the prison visit and had our annual banquet as usual. Everyone received trophies at the celebration. Coach spoke about humility and pushing our level of success, once again, to the next season. This time things will be a little bit different for us. Our team had been very successful, but we were really small as a team. There were several key players who could have been playing on the pound below us because of their age. A few could have played down two pounds. The next pound was the last one being the 120 lb. This was the one that you could play on for two years. So now for the first time, we were going to have to merge with the returning players, already playing on the 120 lb. Most of those guys were 13-14 years old. The majority of our team members were 11-12 years old. This meant we would be very young next season and really small. Some players had a tough decision to make, whether to stay down and play on the 110 lb again or move up with us.

Come on continue to roll with the Colts to Chapter 6 to see what went down with the 120 lb Squad.

**Crestwood Colts 110 lb Team**

## Chapter 6
## The first 120 lb

With our fourth football season in the books, the Colts go right back into basketball. We played in the Irondale league, and it was very competitive. Just like on the football team, over time we seem to learn one another on the basketball court to gel as a team. This particular season there would be no stopping us on the court. We lost one game during the season; however, we managed to bounce back to win the rest of our games including the championship. Everyone enjoyed playing basketball and the year that we had. If you asked me, the whole team thought they were supposed to be the MVP. It was a great experience, lots of fun, and it added to the unbreakable bond that our team shared.

Next, we rolled into the summer of 1988, and we're all excited that school is out. Coach Daryl strikes up another trip with the team. This time it would be a second camping trip. No, we didn't go back to Mt. Cheaha. This trip was at a camping site near six flags in Atlanta, Georgia. The month was June, so there was not going to be a need for players to come back early because of snow and cold weather. The camping site was a very short stay from Six Flags, so both mornings we were the first people to arrive at the Amusement Park. As soon as the gates open, we flooded in locating our favorite rides. Arriving this early was awesome, because normally at Six Flags there is always a long line to ride the rides. We enjoyed a fun field Friday and Saturday at Six Flags during the day, and at night we spent time at the cabin site: Lots of laughs, fun, games, and unforgettable memories.

The fun and games wouldn't last long because now it's July and the first 120 lb season is now upon us. Coach

Darryl knew that this would be our biggest, and most challenging season so far. One of the reasons it was such a challenging season is because our previous 120 lb coach had left to coach Center Point. No big deal right; however, he took most of the team with him that was supposed to stay for their second season and play with us. Typically, the 120 lb team would be filled with second year players who are 13 and 14-years-old. At least half of the team anyway. This particular season most all of the other 120 lb team in the league was stacked with second-year players. So here we are moving up to this level, and only eight players were going to stay back to join our team. The guys that remained were Bernardo Calhoun, Patrick Brackens, DeMond Mcconico (Pooh), Anthony Allen, Terrail Craig, Richard Eaton, and Lorenzo Ford. Besides not having many players returning, we also had another problem on our hands. Remember our team had players who by rule, could stay back and play again on the 110 lb because of their age. One of the key players who decided to stay down and play was our quarterback, Wilson. Despite the fact that Wilson was staying back, Coach Daryl continued to coach the 120lb team. The next impact player to stay down was T.J. who was our starting offensive guard. He also played defensive line and fullback. T.J. even kicked off for us on special teams. Another player who stayed down was Randy. Not only did Randy stay down but he left Crestwood and went to Center Point with Coach Mark. He was going to play on their 110lb team. Randy was one of the fastest backs in the league but played behind Cam at wingback. I think his family wanted him to be the feature back, which he was due, so they left Crestwood. Finally one of the best players in the league was not returning who was our fullback and linebacker, Andy. He probably led the entire league in touchdowns for four years, and he was a fierce hitter. Andy was right on the weight limit each year. His parents decided not to try and keep his weight down, but to go ahead and prepare him for high school ball. That was a great deal of productivity and tons of experience not returning to the team. Keep in mind that we sometimes called our plays from the line of scrimmage or got the hand signals from Coach, so to lose one of your quarterbacks would be critical. In all, we lost two dynamic running backs, a quarterback, and a tough offensive lineman who opened holes for those two backs. Also on defense, we lost one of our corners, Charles Stephens.

So as practice started, we tried to blend the returning eight players into our system. After weeks of training, the team was beginning to shape up. Our coaches did a nice job with filling our vacant slots with the returning eight guys. Bernardo was working out at quarterback and ultimately would get the second string job behind James. Patrick and Demond were playing at defensive end. Pooh filled one of the running back slots. Anthony (Peanut) played defensive line and linebacker. Terrail played on the offensive line. Richard was working out at corner, and Lorenzo would replace Andy at fullback and play corner on defense. It was kind of difficult early on because the guys had to learn the plays and our terminology. These guys were all great players so eventually they adapted well. Ford and Mcconico had learned some of the offensive plays in the backfield and were doing great. Once again the defense was fast, and tough, but small in size. Our offensive line was tough, but considerably small in size, as well. Our entire team as a whole was small.

After a few weeks of practice, Coach accepted a practice game request against Tarrant. This was the same coach who had wanted to beat us badly. The day of the scrimmage, the guys from Kingston were at Chubb's house waiting for the bus. Coach pulled up, and everyone is there except Lorenzo. Coach was very big about being on time, but he waited a few minutes to see if Lorenzo would show up. Coach ended up leaving to continue on our normal pickup route and said that Ford would have to get his way to the park. We arrived at our park, and there is still no sign of Ford. Coach Tim inserted Mcconico in at the fullback slot. Coach Love had to make some adjustment on defense because Ford was going to start at corner. So we are loading up on the Green Machine at Crestwood Park and headed out toward Tarrant. We are followed by the Mom Squad and all of our fans. Everyone wanted to see what our team was going to look like this year without a lot of key players. Also, everyone knew that this was our first year on the 120 lb team. The last thing was that lots of people knew that the majority of our 120 lb from the previous year was now at Center Point. We arrived at Tarrant field, and it was already jam-packed. A lot of other teams are also there watching. Tarrant had a stacked second-year team with lots of experience. We went through our normal routine and got ready to weigh in. Coach Daryl made the decision to allow all of Tarrant players to play without weighing in. He said it's just a scrimmage game, let them all play. I think this one came back to bite us by allowing everyone to play. Tarrant went behind the shed for several minutes and came back out ready to play. They had a lot of players that had grown a few inches and gained a lot of weight. Wow!! That was the fastest growth spurt and weight gain program I'd ever seen in my life. There was no way that these were the same boys that were previously standing in line to weigh in. We knew our team would be small but not this small. If you could have seen the size difference, it looked like we didn't belong on the field with these guys. They went on defense first after the kickoff. Our offense started on about the thirty-five-yard line. I was on the kickoff receiving team and had just made it to the sideline. I took my helmet off and took a knee. All of our parents were cheering but with a very concerned look on their faces. They had to be thinking, will all of our games be this lopsided in size. So on our first play from scrimmage, James walks up to the line to call the play. Just get a visual of this: our largest offensive lineman would have been the smallest player on their defensive line. James yells out- ready- team down-sed- hike. All you heard was a loud lick, and the coaches yelling defense. I thought to myself, "Oh boy, this is gonna be a long day." We fumbled the ball due to a missed assignment on the offensive line; Mike was hit hard. The mix up came exactly where we lost T.J. from left guard. It was only the first play, and we were feeling the effects of missing players. Once the defense got on the field in the huddle, Mike who also played linebacker was still trying to knock off the cobwebs from the hit. I was at the left safety spot in our cover two defense. On their first play on our 35-yard line, they ran a reverse to the opposite side of the field. Their receiver got outside containment and headed toward the end zone. I'm trailing the play running across the field trying to save the score. The wide receiver from the opposite side of the field peels back and takes me off my feet. This woke me up very quickly. Their player made it down to the four-yard-line on their first play. It was first and goal from the four-yard-line. They had a huge fullback who was their go-to guy. On first down, we stopped them on the two yard line. Now, second and goal from the two, we stopped them on the one-yard-line. Third and goal from the one, and we held them to no yards. And then it was fourth and goal from the one. I can still see the play. ToJo and Mike who were the two inside linebackers were in the A gaps on the line of scrimmage. All of the other nine defenders were down on the line except for the two safeties Chubb and I. We knew who was getting the ball, their big back #42. The play starts, and he is lined up behind two lead blockers. They gave it to him, and we met right at the line. I hit him low, and Chubb hit him high. And we're under the bottom of the pile. I'm laying on the goal line, and #42 was on top of me. The referees came in after the scuffle and showed no touchdown signal. I thought we made a hell of a goal line stance; however, they gave them the score. We stopped the extra point so they led 6-0. Our defense is ticked off, but we continued to play. We went back on offense, and it was more of the same. Our line could not move them off the ball and had trouble running. Man, we were missing that team chemistry and also missing our new starting fullback Ford. We managed a few first downs, but we just could not punch one in. The second quarter started, and it was still 6-0. We tried to mix it up and throw the ball more, but they were putting a lot of pressure on James. They were hitting James on every play. A lot of the hits were very late, several seconds after the ball was gone. Our fans were complaining to the referees about it; however, they turned a blind eye to it. It was getting out of control. James could release the ball and four to five seconds after that he would get hit and picked up and thrown down to the ground. Coach Daryl and all of the coaches were complaining. On defense we were small, but we were hitting. Two, three, and four guys was on every play. One play their running back got outside and was on his way to the end zone. It was the same scenario I saw on the first play of the game, but this time there would be no crack back on me. I caught their tailback on the far sideline and took him under the bleachers saving the score.

All you heard was (ooooh) from the crowd. There was dirt, mud, and everything on my face after that one. Again the defense held them out of the end zone to no score. At halftime, the score is still 6-0. During halftime, the concern from our parents grew even more. Especially Ms. Laura Ann, who is the mom of James. I think all of our parents wanted to stop the game seeing how big they were, and how the game was being called or in our case not called. Sometimes they were piling up on our backs after we were already down. And oh yeah they were talking tons of trash to us. On one particular play, To-Jo hit #42 while running up the middle with one of his fierce licks. I was coming up behind him and saw the whole play. Anyone else probably would have stayed down, but #42 got up and said, "That's all y'all got." His voice sounded like he was at least 18 years old. During the second half, it was more of the same with them hitting James. We kept fighting and continued to keep them out of the end zone. The problem was we couldn't get one in the end zone. The score still 6-0 headed to the fourth quarter. At this point our parents are on the sidelines and almost on the field. I 'll never forget what happened next. We called a roll out pass play to ToJo and Terrail. James rolled out and threw the ball away because he didn't have time. Literally, five seconds after the ball was gone, the defenders hit James and picks him up and drops him on the ground. No flag was thrown on the play. We're screaming and hollering, Coach has now gone berserk yelling and cursing the refs. At this point, we cleared the benches and ran over to James pushing and shoving which turned into a brawl. Next thing we know Ms. Laura Ann is headed on the field with a 22 pistol gun. I mean she was literally 10 yards on the field walking swiftly toward the officials. She was furious and for good reason, I mean that was her son they had been hitting late the whole game. Our coaches had to grab her and take her back off the field. She was cursing along with everyone in green and white. Man, it was total pandemonium out there. I mean did people want to see us lose this bad? At this point, our sidelines were ready to pack it up and leave, but we continued to play. The game resumed, but you can tell that they were going to do anything to keep that 6 point lead. We held up on defense the last quarter, keeping them to their lone score. Our offense had the ball last with one drive to try and tie or win the game. We reached their 45-yard-line with one play left. We had to maximum protect, meaning to keep most of the players in to block. James released a Hailmary pass to the end zone. Will the Saffo "Bomb" work this time similar to the what worked on the 75 lb team? The ball is in the air, and both of our receivers were knocked down before they could make a play on the ball. No flag thrown, as they run off the field with a 6-0 win. Coach and all of our assistants are yelling and screaming. No handshakes from our opponents as they storm off the field in celebration. Everyone on our sideline is shocked but yet furious. Coach Daryl's Crestwood Colts lost a scrimmage game. You would have thought we had lost a regular season game the way people was acting. I'm not the one to complain, but that game was going to be very difficult for us to win either way. We fought and battled all the way to the last second. After the game, Coach talked to us about the game, as all of the parents were still upset about the calls and noncalls. The officials are on the opposite side of the field with them laughing and joking. Coach tells all of us that we will be fine when the season starts.

The word about this game traveled extremely fast. Before we can get back to our neighborhoods good, everyone was talking about the game. All we heard from people was, man I heard Tarrant killed y'all. Their talking like the score was 35-0. They had no idea of what happened during the game. It seems as if everywhere we went, people were talking about this loss. I heard it even at the barbershop. The word on the street was that our dynasty was over.

Next, we headed back to practice and work on some of the mistakes we made. Lorenzo was back to take on that fullback position. We battled for the right to wear the green jerseys. This was new to our eight new guys on the team; however, they adapted, fell right in and loved the competitive practices. We finished up the preseason practices and were ready for the season. Will the season be like that practice game we had? Will our small size be a problem all year for us?

Our season started with jamboree games that were located at Center Point Park. We were scheduled that evening to play Central Park first, then Center Point after that. It was a rainy Saturday in which the rain had came down all day. The field was very saturated by that evening. We pulled up in the Green Machine with just our green Crestwood t-shirts and shorts. We didn't even have game pants on at the time. We headed up the hill to go weigh in. Both Central Park and Center Point were extremely larger than us. The eight new guys are staring across at what was their teammates the previous year on Center Point's team. Both teams were talking trash, laughing at us about the practice game we lose, and joking about our team size. Coach tells all of us to be quiet and don't say anything back. Now we can't wait to get back to the bus and change. After the weigh-in, we headed back to the bus to strap up. We're are chanting, pissed off and ready to roll. Coach comes on the bus and fires us up even more before we go out. Despite the wet and muddy conditions, the Mom Squad is there wearing their ponchos and rain boots. Like

I mentioned earlier, they were at every game, no matter what. As we jogged back up the hill in a single file line, all you could hear was the sounds of our cleats beating against the pavement. We get to play Central Park first, and again it seems as if they are twice our size. The rain had ceased, but the field was still very wet. We go on defense first, and I'm playing the left safety spot and our cover two defense. Lorenzo is on my side at the left cornerback spot. On Central Park's first play from scrimmage, their tight end went out for a pass called a ten and out. He ran underneath me but behind Lorenzo. The play was blown dead by the officials because of a false start penalty. Their receiver was about 6 feet tall and huge. Now as their team walked back to their side of the ball, Central Park never went back into the huddle to call a new play. So I went over to Lorenzo and said, did you see what they are trying to do? He's coming under me and behind you. Granted he has about 6 to 7 inches in height on both of us; there was no way we could jump with him to high point the ball. I tell Lorenzo, if they come at us and throw it up to the big boy, I was going to hit him low and told Ford to hit him high. Ford says, "Alright 'C,' I Gotcha Dogg." Just like we said, they came right at us. This is the first play, so I was still dry, and the field was soggy wet. I slid over some to the right and baited the quarterback as if I didn't know where the play was going. Their quarterback released the ball up high, the receiver goes up, and I timed the hit perfectly. I went low and took the guy's legs out. Now I'm soaked even down to my underwear. The receiver is on top of me. Water was on my face as I hear the roar and rumble of the crowd. I'm thinking, "Man, Lorenzo had to have cleaned this guy's clock. Funny thing was while I'm getting the guy off of me, I could still hear the crowd cheering. As I get the water out of my eyes to look up, while still lying on the grass, all I could see was #42 going up the sidelines with the ball. Ford had intercepted the ball off of my hit. That was not the game plan we talked about!!! I was 38 hot at him. Here I am soaking wet, and he is running an interception back up the field. So I get up running toward him. Everyone else ran to him congratulating him and giving him high fives. Ford is on offense, so he tries to hurry up and get to the offensive huddle. I know he sees me coming. I caught him before he could make it. When I get there, I'm like, "What in the hell were you doing man! You were supposed to have hit him high." He answers, "Well when you cleaned him, the ball popped up and was just sitting there, so I just grabbed it. I'm like, "Man, I don't want to hear that sh%t." We still laugh about that play today. Our offense went down and finished the drive with a score. The defense was again stellar, keeping them out of the end zone. Despite their size, all of the pregame talking, we won the game 14-0. You could tell right away that all of our games were going to be difficult this season.

Next, we moved on to play Center Point. Again they had a lot of our former players on their team. They were big, fast, and loaded with talent. So we started the second game, and we went on defense first. We stopped them on their first drive. They came right back and held our offense on the first drive. This game was going to be a good one. We continued to trade drives and stops on both sides for most of the game. Mike finally broke loose on a 30-yard-run placing the ball on their 15-yard-line. Cam would take a reverse in the end zone to score, and we went up 6-0 late in the fourth quarter. Our defense held them on their final attempt to score. To-Jo tipped a pass that was intercepted by Chubb to secure the win. So much for all of the talk before the game. So much for "Crestwood is gonna be sorry this year." So much for us being too small. We came out the gate against two of the top teams in the league at 2-0. Center Point easily could have been the best team in the league coming into the season.

We headed back to practice and continued to get better and work on our craft. We looked at some things we needed to work on from the first two games. It was very clear that we were going to be smaller than our opponents. We had to utilize our team speed to cover for the lack of size. The defense was practicing getting everyone to the ball. Our offense continued to cross and trap block to help with the run game. James and Bernardo were throwing the ball well. Terrail, Billy, and To-Jo were catching passes from the quarterbacks. We were rugged, tough, relentless and ready for whatever we had to face the rest of the way. We were picked to finish sixth in the league this year. We came out with a chip on our shoulders. The Colts are still the four-year reigning undefeated champs. How are people picking us to win only half of our games? The next game was against Adamsville. They were a good team with a super talented quarterback. We had to gang tackle him and tried to keep him in the pocket. Mike, Lorenzo,, Mcconico, and Cam were running hard. Verdell and Reg were rolling at the defensive end. Jesse, Munt, James, Anthony, and Patrick were shoring up the defensive line. To-Jo and Mike were at the inside linebackers spot-hitting. Richard and Lorenzo were on the corners. Chubb, Cam, and I were some ball-hawking safeties. We downed Adamsville 24-6 to remain undefeated. For the next three games, we stayed perfect, getting close wins to remain undefeated. All of these games went into the fourth quarter before being decided. Our next game was scheduled against Huffman at our place. They were also undefeated and had an outstanding team. They were led

by running back Santana and on defense by their
defensive end Mario Manning  Mario became and is still a
good friend of mine who ended up being my teammate
later at Woodlawn High.This was the premier matchup of
the week. We had a good week of practice battling for the
green jerseys. That Friday night we all went over to
Coach's house to spend the night.  We watched film on
Huffman and saw their talented backfield. One of them was
very tall and fast. Their defense looked solid as well. So
later that night we were playing around, joking and cutting
up. Some of the guys, like To-Jo, were teasing Wilson
about how his sisters were so pretty. Wilson did not like
that at all.  He warned the fellas to stop, but they continued.
Wilson got so mad that he eventually pulled his pistol out
of frustration. I think the guys got the message then.
Eventually, he cooled down and put the gun back upstairs
with no harm to anyone. We never did tell Coach about it.
No one wanted Wilson to get in trouble with Coach. The
next morning we got up and watched some more film of
Huffman.  We were trying to get in all we could before the
game. Since we played the last game of the day, the field
was jammed packed. People who were with the 75 lb and
85 lb team even stayed or came back to watch this one.
There were people, literally, everywhere around the field.
They were all up on the playground and tennis courts.
Finally, we see them up close at the weigh-in.  They are
bigger in person versus what the tape showed. The tall
running back looked even taller standing by him. We get
on the bus chanting and getting fired up. Once we exited
the bus, it was so crowded that they had to make a lane for
us to come down the hill to the field. James stopped and
picked up his burger (like always) from his mom right
before entering the gate. So the game starts, and it was
very loud.  In five years, up to this point, this had to have

been the loudest crowd I had ever heard.  Huffman brought a large cheering crowd with them. We battled back and forth without a score from either team. You could see both crowds running up and down the sidelines on every play. Our Moms Squad is cheering and chanting.  It was 0-0 in the second quarter when Coach Love dialed up a safety blitz on my side. We ran a stunt with the defensive lineman and linebacker with the safety blitz.  Huffman had the right play call for the blitz. I got picked up on the safety blitz, and we had two guys that collided during the stunt. They ran a jet sweep to their tailback who took it to the house. Huffman scores first and gets the two-point conversion.  We didn't get to punch one in so at halftime we trailed 8-0. We were in a dogfight. Everyone on our sidelines had looks of concern on their faces. Could this be the first game we finally go down?  Huffman's sidelines were loud and seemed pretty confident. Our coaches talked to us during half-time about continuing to fight and not giving up. Seems like everything we tried in the first half, they had an answer for it. The third quarter started, and both teams were driving the ball down the field, but having to punt. It was going to be tough to score on both of these defenses.  James finally led the offense down at the end of the third quarter for our first score. James hit Terrail on a 30-yard touchdown pass. We missed the two-point conversion making the score Huffman 8, Crestwood 6. "Fourth quarter, our quarter!" chants erupted from the field to our sidelines.  During this time Coach talked to us about staying the course, and also these types of games are why we practice so hard.  Huffman drives down the field on their next possession, but we hold them on a fourth and one play to get the ball back. Our next possession we get the ball back and had a good drive going, but only to fumble it back to Huffman. They had the ball up 8-6 with about four minutes left. Of course, we assume they were going to run the ball to kill the clock. Coach Love told the defense that we needed one more stop to give our offense one more chance to win. We stopped them from getting a first down on first, second, and third down and they were looking at a fourth and three attempt. Huffman decided to punt and pin us deep in our own territory. With all of our timeouts remaining, we could still run or throw the ball. James led a drive mixed with short passes and draw plays to keep the chains moving. The fans on our sideline were cheering louder than ever. We reached the 50-yard-line with one minute and 30 seconds left. On the next play, Huffman sent a blitz, and the perfect play was called. Lorenzo caught a screen pass and took the ball down to the 20-yard-line. Coach called a timeout but we were now in scoring range. This was a crucial decision for Coach to make. Do we play for a field goal attempt or try to score? Since we had timeouts remaining, Coach decided to go for the touchdown. Huffman defense stopped the next play as the time is winding down. Third down comes and Mike breaks loose off tackle for a score. Our fans are yelling and screaming. The sidelines are going nuts. We're up 12-8 with only 12 seconds left. They stopped our two-point conversion after the score. Next, our coaches talked with the kickoff team and warned us to look for a reverse. Also, they told us to stay in our lanes as we run down the field. We followed our orders and stayed in our lanes during the kickoff to stop them. Huffman had one last play to throw a Hailmary pass. They rolled out and heaved one up a bit, and we knocked the ball down to secure the win. WHEW!!! We won the dogfight battle 12-8. Both teams played their hearts out. Both teams were going to have something to say come playoff time. Our fans were chanting, "Who dat talkin' 'bout beating them Colts, who dat who dat, say what!" We are all chanting and celebrating. And there they were, the Moms Squad with the cheerleaders singing, "We are proud of you, and we are proud of you." Huffman was a very good team and gave us one of the best games we had played in five years. So Coach Daryl's Colts starts out 5-0 on the season when everyone predicted that we would only win five games total. The league even predicted we would finish in 5th or 6th place. After we defeated Huffman, a well needed and a well-deserved bye week was upon us. We were totally exhausted after that one.

Before we could take time off and recuperate, the Colts were hit with a tragedy of a teammate. Patrick, one of our defensive ends was shot and killed in my neighborhood the next week. So instead of us having a week off, we had to attend a funeral of our teammate. Coach was devastated to hear the news. Here is a man that had done so much to keep us off the streets and out of trouble, and the worst of the worst incident happened. The murder of Patrick was even more heartwrenching for the guys like myself, Lorenzo, Chubb, Munt, and Anthony because we were all from Kingston just like him. To make the things even more difficult, I saw the event when it took place. Lorenzo and I were hanging out in the neighborhood across the street from the altercation. Apparently, Patrick had been beating up on this guy a couple of times before that day. Earlier that afternoon, the guy had been saying that if Patrick continued to bully and pick on him, that he was going to kill him. We didn't take him seriously, so we thought that he was just talking. Later that evening both guys were headed towards each other at an intersection but couldn't see one another coming. From where I was standing, I knew they were about to meet. Patrick was walking with a friend, and the other guy was walking alone.

When they met, Patrick's friend says, "There that ni##a go over there, why don't you go over to him and slap him?"

*(Young men and women please don't fall for negative peer pressure. Parents, please talk with your kids about their choices. Kids, if you are getting peer pressure to do something wrong, please walk away, and talk to your parents or any responsible adult, whether it's a teacher, coach, or a policeman).*

Patrick took his friend's advice and walked right up to him and slapped the guy in the face. All of a sudden the guy pulls out a gun, Lorenzo and I took off running around the block in the opposite direction. Seconds later, we hear the shots. So we continue to run until we reach safety. One thing I know is that stray bullets don't have any names on them. Moments later everyone in the projects came out of their homes to see what happened. Then the police, fire truck, and ambulance are all on the scene. The local news station made their way out and seemed like the entire neighborhood was out there. We made our way back to the scene, and I see my teammate lying there shaking on the ground. His brains were blown out on the sidewalk. He passed away on the way to the hospital. The Colts spent that next Saturday funeralizing our teammate. We decided to dedicate the rest of the season to him.

Back at practice that following Monday, we started like normal with stretching and two laps around the field. After the two laps, we would typically split up into individual positions to work on techniques. This particular Monday was different. Coach got all of us together, and we took the whole time we were supposed to practice and just talked. We talked about choices, our decisions, peer pressure, and bullying. Coach asked us if anyone was being a bully or being picked on at school or in the neighborhoods. He pleaded for us to tell him or come to him after practice and speak one on one. Hearts were heavy as we continue to think of our teammate and discuss life's situations. A few guys that were dealing with issues at home and or school did go to Coach after the talk. You just never know what people and especially young people are dealing with. Some were having issues in their own homes or with their parents. If a parent is not present in the home, or if abuse is in the home, this can have a great impact on a kid's life. All of our coaches opened up themselves to the players so that they could be there for us if we needed them for any situation. Some shared their stories to let us know that they had dealt with issues as well. This was probably the best practice we ever had, and it didn't have anything to do with football; it was simply just about life.

So next we move on to the second half of the season and were back focused on continuing to get better. We continue to win close games week after week. The Colts steamrolled past our next four opponents to place us at 9-0. We had one game left in the regular season and guess who was coming to town. You guessed it right - Tarrant. The team that beat us in the scrimmage game at the beginning of the season. Keep in mind that our star fullback didn't play in that practice game at their place. Also, we found out that back during the scrimmage when Coach decided not to weigh-in, they played some guys from their freshman team, junior varsity, and one guy from their high school varsity team. I will tell you in a moment on how we found out about the varsity player that played against us. All week we practiced hard and had a great gameplan for Tarrant. We also found out why their coach wanted to beat us so bad. We were told that allegedly he was making bets that his team would beat us. Word also got out that even before this upcoming game he called and tried to bet our coach on who would win. Our coach never did anything like betting on any games. Their coach called a nearby sports store in error trying to reach our coach. The store owner told him, "Man you have the wrong number to reach Coach Daryl, plus he's not going to bet you anyway. But hell I'll bet you Crestwood don't lose to y'all." So the store owner allegedly took the $500 bet with their coach. Tarrant coach says don't you know we are the only team that beat them. The store owner replies, that was a scrimmage game, we will see this Saturday. So after the Friday night practice Coach gets everyone weighed to monitor which players had to be watched that night. Anyone who weighed 117 lb or higher was considered a high risk for making the 120 lb team limit the next day. Those players food intake had to be closely observed. There were only a few guys that had to be checked. The guys got in a single file line waiting to get on the scale. I snuck into the equipment room and got in line with them, only weighing about 100 pounds. Coach had his back turned and didn't see me sneak in. After one of the players got checked, he said next but didn't turn around. He was focused on the scale. So I hop on the scale, and the needle didn't move at all. Coach turned around looked and said, "Ah hell Corey, you can weigh in tomorrow with all of your pads and helmet on and still make the weight limit." We all laughed at that one. Lorenzo got on the scale next and checked in at 116 pounds. Coach considered him to be fine and placed him with the players that did not have to watch their food intake that night.

After all of the weight checks, we leave the park and head to Coach Daryl's house to spend the night, our usual ritual. We got over there and watched some game film, played around, and watched television. Mrs. Becky had all kinds of food for us to eat: chicken fingers, pizza, fries, and corn dogs were some of the goodies. We ate well all night including Lorenzo. We even ate ice cream with hot fudge syrup on top for dessert. There wasn't anyone who could say they were hungry. However all of the heavyweights would plead the fifth about that. They had to enjoy a nice big delicious salad. I still say those guys use to sneak in a fry or two sometimes. So later that night we are watching Fox 6 to see the high school sports highlights. Mike's older brother Patrick (P.T.) was playing high school ball, and we were trying to see if he was going to be on the news. P.T. was always at all of our games. We did see him in action catching a touchdown pass. After that, we saw something that blew us all away. We saw the same guy who scored the only touchdown against us in that practice game against Tarrant, playing for their high school. Wait a minute, here! We told Coach to come look at what we were yelling about. The player took his helmet off and had that same number 42 and everything. The announcer on the news said, "Tarrant junior, fullback scores on a five-yard touchdown run. We all said simultaneously "JUNIOR! " No wonder he was so much bigger than us in that game. Seeing this junior on the news confirmed for us that we were not counting that lost, especially the way they treated us over there.

Saturday morning arrived, and we got up eating bacon, eggs, grits, sausages, pancakes, the whole nine yards. We packed all of our things and thanked Mrs. Becky and family for their hospitality. Later that evening it was getting close to game time. We weighed-in at half-time of the 110 lb game, and the park was jam-packed. I thought the Huffman game was crowded. Oh My God! This was like an Alabama versus Auburn game in youth sports.

Everyone knew that this was the only team to defeat us in five years in that scrimmage game. I think a lot of people came to witness our first real lose. People were packed in the park like someone was giving away free money. On the opposite side of our field, where the visitors sit, is a highway called Crestwood Boulevard. Cars were lined up all the way down the highway. I can't express enough about the magnitude of this game. Tarrant weighed in first and was all fine. We go next, and up to myself at #23 we were fine. I look back and see Mike, #33, and we were still fine. After Mike came out, the coaches shut the door. This normally meant that someone had to strip down to their shorts to make the weight limit. James was usually right on the weight mark each week. Could it be possible that we would have to play without our quarterback? Remember Wilson is on the 110 lb this year. Instead of it being James, #44, who they were checking, it was Lorenzo, #42. He had to strip down to his underwear to try and make it. He got on the scale, and it was right at 120 pounds. Their coach told him to take a deep breath and raise his hands above his head, after that the scale went up a small notch. NO, NO, NO their coach yelled, He can't play, He's overweight. Our coach goes off because he made it the first time before being told to do those things. Unfortunately, the AYFL commissioner said the rules are that the opposing coach weighs and makes the decision if a player is overweight and cannot participate. After those requests they gave him, it tipped the scales maybe an ounce. The bottom line was they had seen him play and didn't want him in the game. Coach was devastated because they wanted to exclude Lorenzo strategically. Our coach always allowed all players to play, no matter what the child's weight was. The bad blood continued with these two teams. James steps up next, and he did make the weight. Everyone else was fine after that. I guess they got who they wanted out of the game. Now we're all sitting on the bus joking and playing around as usual. We see Ford coming back without his game pants on. We are wondering, what is going on. I 'm saying to myself he weighed 116 last night after practice last night. I know he made the weigh in. I was wrong. Coach comes on the bus and confirms the bad news. So here we go a second time playing these guys without one of our star players. The hurt and pain in coach's voice were difficult to listen to. He broke down that day talking to us again about life. He stated that in life you will face people who will cheat, lie, and do anything to get ahead of you. He said that sometimes you don't even have to do anything to them. That's just the world we live in. He said trials and tribulations will come; he said just always continue to do what's right and fight like hell. This was the first time we saw coach in tears before a game. He left and went out to talk with our assistant coaches to make offensive and defensive changes to the starting lineup. I'm wondering who will be my left corner in our cover two defense. Mcconico took on the fullback spot who was also very powerful and fast. While on the bus putting on the rest of our equipment, Coach came back to let us know it's time to play. Usually when he came back we would always still be horseplaying around. After we saw our coach hurt, that really pissed us off. From the 75 lb team's first game and at all of our home games, we all would walk down the ramp to the field holding our helmets in our hand. That was because of the pregame individual introduction. After hearing Coach speak to us in tears, the whole bus was silent. All you could hear were the sniffles of players out of anger. There was no talking and playing around this time. Without anyone saying anything, we began getting ready and within minutes we were fully dressed with our helmets already on. All you heard was the snapping of chinstraps. We were standing up, dressed, and in numerical order ready to roll. Coach came back on the bus about to say come on guys let's get ready; it's time. However, we were already ahead of him. The look on coach face was saying I can't believe they are all ready. Coach had never seen us ready in all of the five years. Everyone on that bus had eyes full of water. We exited the bus with our fist balled up and tears still coming down our face. People were standing outside the bus waiting for us to come out. Some of them were out there making bets; I still remember that after seeing our faces, one guy ran and doubled his bet with another person. He ran to the other side yelling "Crestwood ain't losing today!" As we made it closer to the field, there was James's mom with his meal. James was so laser focused that he walked right past her; this was also a first in five years. His mom was so shocked that she took a bite out the hamburger saying, "Oh hell what is going on." Very soon the word had spread that Ford was not playing in the game. After warming up in the end zone another first happen. As the announcer called the first player's name Billy Latham, #10, we all ran out on the field to our sidelines. We were ready to roll baby. We won the toss and elected to go on defense first. Coach Love called the kickoff team over to him for a quick huddle. He was so intense and he was firing us up. We started chanting, "What we gone do - do it to em- what we gone do - do it to em - strike that match - Fire it up- what we gone do - do it to em." He us told to move our feet. We all paused because normally that meant we were to run in place and get ready to dive on the ground on our stomachs. Obviously, he didn't want us to do that before the game started. The field was dirty from some light rain earlier that day. After we hesitated, he screamed move your damn feet!!! We all started to chop it up quickly. Coach Love yells hit it. We follow the orders and lay out in the dirt. We did this a couple of times before stopping. So now here we are dirty, grimy, fired up and ready to kickoff. It was funny to see their faces when they saw us coming on the field already dirty. They were sparkling clean, and we were the nasty dogs. I walked past Ford and said, "We gotcha Dogg and Imma get the first lick for you, Man." I was the safety valve on the kickoff team and didn't normally sprint down the field, just in case someone broke free. This game I lowered my hand to release everyone else down the field then turned and sprinted right behind them. They ran the return to our sideline and their runner jumped up trying to avoid a hit from a flying To-Jo. I caught him right under the chin. What a way to start the game. I looked up at Ford, confirming my pre-game words with a head nod. The crowd is rocking and the game is on. I think we were too excited because the defense had a breakdown and made an assignment error on their first drive. We were showing a cover three  defense but was suppose to have rolled into a cover two on the snap.  Somehow they ran a play action pass play, and one of our guys forgot to roll into the cover two.  Their receiver was wide open as they struck first on a 30-yard touchdown. Tarrant strikes first but we stopped their extra point attempt,  leaving the score 6-0. Just before the half, Cam broke loose and scored to tie the game at 6-6. The game goes back and forth without a score through the third quarter. Our defense rallied after that first score and locked them down the rest of the game. Mcconico and Mike scored a touchdown in the final quarter to put us up for good. We won the game by a score of 18-6.

The Tarrant game was another hard fought battle which we came out on top.  We finished the regular season 10-0 and were National League Champs.  Five years straight with no losses going into the playoffs. We were so elated to give Coach that win, especially after what they did before the game during the weigh-in.

We moved to Avondale Park, once again, due to not having any lights at our field. This was always a sign that it was playoff time. Coach Daryl had a great influence on us, but he also influenced the other coaches. We're at practice, and I'm the corner checking my buddy Ford who is at receiver. I'm playing inside technique (not allowing the offensive player inside). One of the coaches that was helping us out forced me to change and play outside. I'm trying to argue with him, and he basically grabbed my arm and moved me outside. We were in between plays when this happened. As soon as we started back up and ran the play, James throws a dart to Ford on a slant pattern inside me. I make the tackle after a 7-yard game and here comes Coach Daryl running toward me yelling "Corey! What in the hell are you doing! Why are you playing outside technique?" I answered back by saying the assistant coach told me to move outside. Coach looked at the assistant, and he says to Coach, "I didn't tell him that." I can't believe he got scared of coach and sold me out. I could have cursed him out after getting me chewed out. Later on, at practice, I had made a couple of tackles, pass breakups, and interceptions. So I'm letting Coach and the entire offense know about it by trash talking. I'm yelling at the offense, "I got this left corner on lockdown." Next thing I know, Coach looks at me smiling as if he was saying we have to shut him up. The next play they ran a toss to my side and seemed like everyone was coming towards me. I mean they were pulling guards, two or three lead blockers, and the runner. So I did the only thing I could do, and that was duck and go low. They all tried to take me out. I got off the ground, and coach was over there grinning. I said,

"Alright I have something for y'all." Coach wasn't always so strict; he did have a sense of humor. As of now, you should know that everything we did was about competition. Thursday was the last day of the week to compete for the green jerseys. Up until that point, the scrimmages are dead even for the offense and defense. We had one drive left for all of the marbles. If the offense scored they win. If the defense keeps them out of the end zone, we win. They were on the 20-yard- line and driving. Next, they get a first down and end up on the 10-yard-line and have a first and goal. Four plays left in practice, after the first three plays it was now fourth in one on the one-yard -line. Ford and I were best friends, but on this day, he had on a blue jersey, and I had on a red jersey. They lined up in a power eye with Ford in the back. We had nine guys on the defensive line, Chubb and I were the only two standing. James took the snap and handed it off to Ford. He leaped over the top, only to get a lick from me on the goal line. Coach came in and dispersed the pile and says "they didn't make it." The defense went nuts, and we won the green jerseys for Friday. If you ask Ford today, he'll swear that he crossed the goal line. Another play we still argue about currently. This practice led us into our first playoff game.

In the first round of the playoffs, we met Leeds again. They gave us a great effort and hard fought battle in the first round. We eventually cruised to a 24-8 victory. This left the semifinals match ups being Crestwood vs. Central Park and Huffman vs. Center Point. We took care of business by beating Central Park 18-12 in a thriller to make it to our 5th straight championship appearance. Center Point beat Huffman to advance for the showdown: Crestwood vs. Center Point. They hadn't lost a game since we beat them at the beginning of the season, 6-0. Remember the guys were mostly Crestwood players the previous year. Their coach is also the same man that coached our 120 lb team when we scrimmaged them as a 100 lb team two years prior. He also showed our coach a lot of cross blocks and trap blocks that we ran. So to say that they knew us well was an understatement. Lawson field was the match up location. The high school field was packed just like a high school team was playing. We come out in all green jerseys, green pants, with black cleats and black gloves. Center Point is in their white jerseys and burgundy pants. Before the game, Coach gave us the same speech that he had been giving us for five years, "Guys the football has a funny bounce and if it doesn't bounce our way tonight be good sports about it." This same old tone was going in and out of our ears. So we start and the game, nip and tuck. Both teams were held scoreless in the first quarter and in the second quarter we held them again. This defense was still nasty. They would punt the ball to us, and Ford loses it in the lights, fumbles the ball, they recover and go in for a touchdown. They got the two-point conversion, and the score went up 8-0 going into the half. We came out and scored on the next two consecutive drives, one by Ford and one by Mike. Both touchdowns got called back. With the score 8-0, they went down to score again and made it 14-0. That was the score going into the 4th quarter. On our first drive, they stopped us, and we had to punt. Coach Love called a great defensive play where we showed a cover three look and rolled into a cover two on the snap. Center Point throws a quick screen, and our right cornerback Richard Eaton jumped the route, intercepts the balls and takes it 50 yards to the house. Cool, we were back in it. Out of nowhere, there was a flag from the opposite side of the field. They called a clip on our player who was running down the field to congratulate Richard. The Center Point player stopped running in front of him because he knew he was too far out from the play. They got tangled up slightly so our pick-six came back. Keep in mind that this took place on the opposite side of the field and about 40 yards behind the play. After that, we could never recover. They went in with a late touchdown. Giving them the win, 20-0. I can't believe it! Five straight undefeated seasons and we get to the finals and lose. This was the game that Coach talked about weekly since the 75 lb team. We had fumbles, 3 touchdowns called back; you name it. Center Point won, and they went crazy. The build-up for us losing was so great that people ran out of the stands onto the field. Players and adults were pointing their fingers at us and cursing us out. Calling us sorry and losers. You would have thought that their whole team had won the lottery. We saw the officials laughing as they left the field. However, we took the loss with dignity, just like Coach Daryl taught us. That picture of the way they acted, as I sat on one knee was stuck in my head. We all had tears in our eyes; some were laid out on the field crying. We had never lost before and didn't know how to handle it. As we walked off the field, everyone in green was crying. There were women, men, kids; I mean everyone. I will never forget that even the cheerleaders were crying. The Mom Squad was crying their hearts out, but still found their way to cheer as we walked out (they were saying, "we are proud of you, and we are proud of you.") with their voices trembling. I don't know how they got those words out with so many tears coming down, but they did. There is nothing in the world like the strength of a woman. Coach congratulated us in the locker room on a great season. No one thought we would win five games, and would be playing in the championship. We were the smaller team in all 13 games that season. We finally had a loss, and it was devastating for us to handle. We get to our banquet and receive trophies. Coach spoke to us about bouncing back from this minor setback and told us that it was just a part of life. He wanted us to enjoy what we had done in the past but also wanted us to regroup and refocus on our final year coming up. He thanked the eight players that stayed with us from the previous season. Finally, one of the parents sang Whitney Houston's - "Didn't we almost have it all, while the championship game was playing on the screen." I don't believe there was a dry eye in the room. A couple of players had decisions to make like myself and Terrail. Our age and weight allowed us to come back the next year, but we were going to the 9th grade. This was still okay for us to finish our last year, but we just couldn't play football for the high school at the same time.

Let's roll over to the final chapter to see how it all ended for Coach Daryl's Colts.

**Crestwood Colts 120 lb Team**

Chapter 7
The Finale

The spring of 1989 approaches and the Colts rolled
back onto the diamond. This particular season was played
at Avondale Park. The league was very good and had
about twelve teams.  We were accustomed to the field
because our playoff football practices were held there.
Baseball players such as Reg, Wilson, Cam, To-Jo, Terrail,
Chubb, Anterio, and Maurico and I were all back. We were
led by our best player, James.  He was a slugger who
could knock them out of the park. James also had a mean
fastball. We continued to migrate over to Coach's house
during this time. This team was always, I mean always in
some kind of competition; whether it was boxing, playing
cards, video games, we were always trying to win at
something.  The baseball season was loads of fun,
energetic, with lots of experiences. We finished the season
10-2 in the regular season. This time we were hot entering
the playoffs, and we went on to win the championship. Our
bond was inseparable; we were one unit. All of us were
eager to head into the upcoming football season with
Coach Daryl.

The 1989 120 lb football team lost some key players to
the high school ball.  Guys such as Bernardo, Richard,
Anthony, and Lorenzo were now all at Woodlawn High.
Terrail and I were also headed to Woodlawn. The
difference was we were only 13-years-old and had the
option to return for our last season with the Colts. I
originally decided to play on the freshman team, not
knowing what Terrail was going to do. One day after
school Lorenzo and I were getting dressed in the locker

room before high school practice. Coach Stearns had given us our equipment, and we were the only two players left in the locker room. We didn't know what was ahead of us at the time. I leaned over on one knee to tie my cleat, and all I saw was that scene at Lawson field from our championship game loss. The picture was so clear seeing Coach Daryl's face after that game. I saw all of those people taunting and belittling us. There was something that was left for me to finish. I couldn't let my last game with Coach have that picture imprinted in my head. I told Ford to go ahead because I was going back for my last year. I gave him my best wishes and stated that I would see him the following season. About the same time, Terrail had also decided to come back. We notified Coach of our decision, and he was thrilled to hear the news.

We went back to play along with the previous 110 lb players that were moving up from the year before. We were back together with quarterback Wilson, and Headhunter T. J. Most of the old team was reunited and ready to roll. T.J. would fall back into the vacant fullback slot. Our backfield was still loaded with Mike, Cam, Chubb, and T.J. Also James was also back at quarterback. They had the same receivers back to throw it all over the yard too. Terrail, To-Jo, and Billy were back catching everything thrown at them. The offensive line had returned: Mauricus, Reg, and Demetrius. The defense was still looking awesome. Players up front were Dennis, Verdell, Reg, Munt, T.J, and Jesse. To-Jo and Mike were still the inside linebackers. Cam, Che, Teddy, Chubb, and I held down the secondary. The 1989 120 lb Colts came back to reclaim our title.

One problem that I encountered was high school basketball workouts, and conditioning began as soon as school started. I went out for the tryouts and made the junior varsity team. This meant that both of my practices would overlap. It also meant that I wouldn't make it back to Kingston to catch my ride on the bus to football practice. Coach Daryl went out of his way (Going For Two) again and made a small personal route for a handful of players. He assigned one of his employees from his machine shop, Kaylou to drive the bus route for him. This allowed Coach to run the smaller route. Coach would come to Woodlawn High and pick up Terrail and I, along with a few other players in his El-Camino. Yep, Coach would cruise in the El- Camino. For my younger generation, this was a utility /pickup vehicle that was produced by Chevy. The front looked like a car, but the back had a flatbed like a truck. It was about five players that sat back there heading to the field.

Anyone who played for Mean Gene Crittenden at Woodlawn High knew that the practices were hard-nosed, viscous, and had lots and lots of running. The Junior Varsity coaches, Steve Moseley and another coach named Darryl conducted business the same way. Most guys after basketball practice would be physically spent. Here I am practicing basketball from 3:30 pm to 5:30 pm, hopping into the El-Camino to head to football practice from 6-8 pm. Coach Daryl would have my football pants, cleats, shoulder pads, and helmet inside the vehicle. After leaving basketball practice, Coach would be waiting outside the gym for me to come out. I would literally wipe my sweat, hop in the back of the vehicle, take off my tennis shoes, slide on my football pants, slip on my cleats and head to another physical practice. These were some long days for a 13-year-old freshman.

*To my kids and Youth of today who are reading this book. This is why there is absolutely NO reason to not get your lesson in school. If I can get up at and leave home at 7am; walk to school from Kingston to Woodlawn, which is approximately 30 minutes or more. After that go through almost eight hours of school, basketball practice, football practice, then get home around 8:30 pm or later every night and still make the honor roll, YOU HAVE NO EXCUSE.*

Back to football practice and this last season would be no different than the others. We were battling for the green jerseys and competing for positions, all over again. It's crazy how we have now played together for six years, and no one was automatically given a position. Coach welcomed all players who requested to try out for a different spot. You had to earn your position each season, no matter what. Each practice was intense because we were eager to remove that taste of defeat from our mouths. For the first time ever, we came into a new season following a loss. After a season with lots of new faces, the chemistry fell right back in place. After the next couple of weeks at practice, we worked hard to get ready for the season. Our first test out the gate was a scrimmage against the Metro League team, A. G. Gaston Bessemer. The Colts loaded up on the Big Green Machine to make the trip down Highway 59 South to Bessemer. This was about a 30 minute drive to the field. We arrived with our entourage behind us. Coach sounded off the signature horn to let everyone know that we were present. People were throwing rocks at the bus, along with cursing and dogging us out. We heard things like, "Y'all are sorry, Centerpoint whipped y'all last year." I thought to myself, "Who do they think they are talking to? Do they not know that we had only lost one game in the whole five years that we played under Coach Darryl. Ok. It's time to show them what time it is." Coach reminded us not to talk back, but to have class and do our talking with our pads on the field. If you combine our last game, the hurt, the tears, the pain, along with these people talking trash. Oh, it's on now! We came out on defense to set the tone. One hard hit after another one, we stopped them on their opening drive. On our first two possessions, Wilson connected with Terrail and Billy for touchdowns to put us up 14-0. We dominated the game on both sides. The defense was lead by Verdell, T.J, James, To-Jo, Chubb, and I. On offense, Mauricus and Leo were opening up holes for Mike, T.J, and Cam. We were leading 44-6 with 3 minutes left in the game when the crowd started throwing bottles on the field. Coach decided that was enough. He became the protector and got us out of there without any injuries. Man, it felt good to get back in the win column. We had a chip on our shoulder that was going to be hell for any team we would face that year.

Two weeks before the season opened Coach took us back to Cherokee Beach. We saddled up on the bus headed out for a little fun in the sun. It was time to let our hair down after weeks of practicing. We ate, played games, swam, and had lots of fun. Even in the water, guys were competing to see who swam the fastest. Some players would cheat and dive into the water too soon. I guess the competition never ended with us, even when we were playing around. Lots of family members, fans, and our cheerleaders came out to have some fun with us. You know we are a little older now, so we enjoyed having the cheerleaders around playing in the sand. The coaches and a few of the dads had their coolers with their beverages in them. We had our Gatorade and water in ours. Everyone was all smiles during and after leaving the beach.

After the beach trip, we were hit with a devastating blow to the team. Each year the week before the season opener, there was the official weigh-in for all teams and all pounds. As I stated earlier every player had to make that official weight to be eligible to play that season. Once the season started, the opposing coach made the weekly decision if the overweight kid would play. However, if you didn't make the official weight check, you had to move up to the next pound or in our case, miss the season. Our quarterback and one of the defensive leaders, James, didn't make the 120 lb official weight check.This was a tremendous lost to the team; losing five years of experience. This meant for the first time; we were not going to have two experienced quarterbacks. This year all of the pressure will be on Wilson, who was up for the challenge. Despite not playing the final season, James still showed dedication and leadership. He came to every game, cheered us on, and encouraged all of his teammates.

When the season started, our first game was against Huffman. This was the team who claimed that they should have beat us the previous year. We won that game 12 to 8 on a last minute drive (chapter 6). This time it would be no dice for Huffman. The Colts rolled to a 50-8 victory right out the gate. We played well on both sides of the ball and in the kicking game. This was the statement game that Coach Daryl's Colts were back. Mike and Cam ran for two touchdowns. Chubb and T.J ran for one. To-Jo and Terrail both caught a touchdown pass from Wilson. Lots of guys contributed on defense including Dennis, Teddy, Che, Munt, and Verdell. The next week was more of the same. We continued playing at a high-level against South Roebuck. After another rough week of practice and preparation, the Colts rolled again to a 28-6 win. This game was tied at the half 6-6. The second half is where we exploded for three scores to break away. After all of our games, we always had our cooler on the sidelines with Gatorade in it. This particular game I guess Coach and a few of the Dads' coolers got mixed up with ours. The Gatorade cooler was up at the top of the stands with the Dads, and their cooler was down on the field. After Coach's post-game speech we all raced over to the cooler. Billy was the first one to the cooler, opened it up and grabbed a cold one. He popped the top, and all you heard from Coach was "Billy put that down son." Billy jokingly responded, "Awww c'mon Coach, I thought these were for us." Coach laughed and said, "Son, give me that beer." Coach Daryl closed the cooler and had the Dads come down with our Gatorade cooler, and they grabbed theirs. We all got a kick out of that. If it wasn't for Coach's quick catch, ol Billy would have took one down. If you ask me, I think he may have gotten a little swig.

Over the next three weeks, we kept our winning streak going making it to 5-0. Coach Daryl continued to check on the guy's school work and home life. After the tragedy we had the previous year, Coach was always concerned about what we were doing in our personal lives. He visited schools to check on players, sometimes unexpectedly. He especially checked on you if a player had received a D or F in their conduct grade. A player not displaying discipline and character was not tolerated on or off the field. The next week Coach showed us what can happen if we didn't make good choices and have discipline as a young man. We took our bye week and re-visited a place we had gone just a few years prior: West Jefferson Prison. We headed there, once again, loading into the Green Machine. Once inside, we talked to the staff and a few inmates. These guys were open, honest, and real with us. They warned us not to ever put ourselves in a position to come there. The inmates talked about our decisions and how quickly things can go wrong. Also, they talked about how sometimes you simply just have to walk away and leave a situation to avoid trouble. They repetitively spoke of watching the company you keep because some were inside simply from being at the wrong place at the wrong time. They continued to state very clearly that everyone is not your friend. We got the opportunity to go back into the cells again and look at their day to day lifestyle. One big guy who was about 6 foot 4 inches tall and weighed about 250 pounds ripped with muscles told us how he had been taken advantage of. He asked us " What do you do if several guys wake u up in the middle of the night with a knife to your throat?" This was another eye opening experience that taught us all valuable life lessons. Coach always taught us to be disciplined in our assignments on the field. He never neglected to teach and show us why it's so important in life to be disciplined off the field.

After the prison trip and a week off the Colts returned to the field for game six against one of our toughest teams: Tarrant. We went to their place, and this is where we played those high school players the previous year in that scrimmage game. Their fan base was loud and rowdy as we pulled up on the bus. This time it didn't appear to be any high school juniors out there. We took care of business with a hard-fought battle, and we won 14-0. Our winning streak kept rolling into game seven against Leeds. We were back at home for an intense matchup with the Greenwaves. Our fans who cheered and chanted each game of the season were awesome. They were just as much or probably more excited than we were. We always had to game plan and stop Leeds talented running back each year. We won the game 18-0. Leeds had a great program but was just not quite great enough to pull off a victory against us during these six years. The mighty Crestwood Colts are flying high and now are 7-0 season headed to a showdown with Central Park. We prepared at practice for another challenging battle. Wilson led the offense which worked hard. Our stable of backs Cam, Mike, T.J and Chubb were having a tremendous season and running strong. They were giving defenses all they could handle. Billy, Terrail, and To-Jo were catching everything in site. Mauricus, Reg and the offensive line dominated up front. Our defense was still rugged and stingy. Munt, Reg, and Verdell kept the D line steady. Mike and To-Jo were hitting machines. Cam, Chubb, Che, Teddy, and I were holding the secondary down. Despite our play, we had another challenge ahead. Central Park was another great team and still looking for their win against Coach Daryl's Colts. That Saturday they came to our place in their blue and gold. Our fans were really pumped up because this was our last regular season home game of the year. The field was packed as usual. The defense came out hitting and setting the tone. We kept their great running back in check. Wilson and the offense were moving the ball mixing the run and pass. Mike and Cam each scored once to lead the way for a 12-0 win to close out the home game finale. This was a fun matchup with both teams having great youth league programs and great fan bases. In the last two weeks of the regular season, we were still taking care of business on the road. Those games were against Pinson and Adamsville. We were able to cruise into the playoffs with two convincing wins 44-0 and 38-6. Everyone got to play in these two games, but in just about every game we played, we all got playing time. I even got to take a few snaps as the third-string quarterback. One reason we were successful is that we had a well-taught, well-coached 2nd and 3rd string player for each position.

We began to prepare for our final playoff appearance as we migrated back to Avondale Park to practice since we didn't have field lights, as you may remember. The first round game was a rematch of the week against Tarrant. We had a great week of practice preparing for the battle. After working hard and finalizing our game plan, we were back at Coach's house that Friday night. We did our normal activities such as eating, playing and watching a film. Everyone refocused on their duties and were ready to get the win. The first round game was played at our field. This time, there would be no doubt about who was the best team. We rolled to a 36-0 blowout at Crestwood Park. T.J and Chubb led the way on offense along with Billy and Terrail hauling in touchdown passes from Wilson. The defense was awesome led by Verdell and To-Jo.

In the semi-final round, we had to face Central Park again. Our game back in week eight and it seemed as if we had just played them. Another week of preparation, film watching and competition made us ready for the challenge. This game was always one of the only games that gave us a scare. They played hard but fell to us 34-6. We celebrated, chanted, and were elated that we were going to our six straight championship game. Six years of undefeated regular season games. Only one loss the previous year and we were back in the finals. Now guess who was waiting on the other side to play us in the finals. You guessed it right, Center Point. This would be a rematch of last years finals. They were extremely talented and also undefeated. They had lots of players that use to be on our team just two years prior. One player was our former running back and defensive back, Randy. He was their star player who was averaging 2-3 touchdowns per game. He was also fast as lightning. Remember he went to Center Point the previous year but stayed down on the 110 lb. For us, this game was like one of our epic green jersey practice battles. However, this would be for all the marbles, one last time. We knew each other well. This was one of the reasons why Terrail and I came back. We wanted revenge badly, and we wanted to send Coach out a winner. People were talking about this game all week. Center Point was confident and for good reason. They were the only team to defeat us in six years.

So now it's the week leading up to the championship game, and we are back at practice. The mood felt very odd knowing that this was the Colts last week of preparation. The field was almost empty due to most of the other pounds being out of the playoffs. We continued our battle for the green jerseys all week. Our defense ran Center Point scheme to give our offense a good look. Also, our offense ran their plays and formations against the defense. Cam was in Randy's position in their offense, who was just as fast as Randy. Thursday practice came around, which was the last one for us in pads, and we went through our normal routine but ended practice prematurely. For six consecutive years after every Thursday practice, we waited to hear who won the week between the offense and defense. This particular Thursday, Coach didn't announce a winner for the first time from 1984-1989. He told us that we were all winners, and on Friday, the offense and defense both will wear the green jerseys. Everyone got the one lap instead of two. Both sides of the ball were to receive Gatorade instead of water. Both sides were to run fewer wind sprints also. We were ready for our final Friday practice before the championship. So Friday comes along, and we were all in green jerseys and helmets. The vibe was great, and we were all excited. The team was loose and full of energy. Each drill was ran with speed and enthusiasm. We went over the game plan, special teams, and goal-line situations. Coach Daryl ended practice early after the wind sprint competition. Ending Friday practices in this way was always a fun and exciting. Plus this was another way to get players to run hard and stay in shape. Coach huddled everyone up and talked to us about the game as well as life. He thanked us for being a special group. Coach also told us it was an honor to be able to teach, coach, and mentor us. He said these memories would last a lifetime. Besides all of this, he reminded us to take all of our experiences we learned over these six years and apply them to our life. When it is taught correctly, football teaches hard work, responsibility, accountability, toughness, competitiveness, how to face opposition, and to always persevere. All of these tools can be utilized at some point in your life. Coach told the team that for some of us, this would be our last time playing organized football. He stated that size, talent, and athletic abilities would not allow some of us to continue on in high school. However, he asked that we use the same principles and efforts that we learned in whatever we do later in life. Coach made a prediction that out of almost 40 players that approximately 20 of us would go on to play high school sports. He stated that seven or eight players would play some type of sport on the collegian level. And finally he predicted that 1 or 2 of us would make it professionally in some sport. He always gave us the honest truth about sports and life. After the practice, we all went to Coach's house to have fun, watch film, and prepare for our last game. We all stayed up all night playing around and enjoying one another. These were good times, and we were truly thankful that the Whittington's opened up their home and hearts to us.

Saturday morning arrives and we were up eating breakfast and watching a little more film before leaving the house. We asked Coach if we could wear all white this year; especially since we wore all green the previous year and lost. Most of the time we wore green jerseys with the white pants or white jerseys with the green pants. He had agreed the year before on our request to wear all green and now he said it would be ok to wear all white later that night. We got to Lawson Field to watch a few of the early games. We were the final game of the night. Man, we were sharp wearing those white jerseys with Crestwood on the front of them in green. Our numbers on the shoulder pads area were also in green. The white pants had the green stripe going down the side. We all had black gloves and black Nike cleats on. Game time came, and all of our coaches were getting us hyped. Love and Tim were shouting, "It's not the size of the dog in the fight - but the size of the fight in the dog - don't come out the gate if you're not ready to fight dog!" The team was in the locker room all jumping up and down. We were chanting, *"Colts get ready to roll - Colts get ready to roll (clap, clap, clap)."* We come out and it's packed on both sides of the field. Our cheerleaders and Moms Squad are out there cheering us on. The cheerleaders held up the banner for us to bust through. Then, something happened for the first time in six years. Coach Daryl burst through the banner first and led us onto the field. Now we are really fired up. The cheerleaders took their place on the sidelines, and the Moms Squad went back into the stands still cheering. Center Point wore their burgundy jerseys and pants with black and white stripes. People were betting and talking lots of trash about who was going to win. We kicked off and went on defense first. The very first play of the game, they ran Randy around the right end. Reg strung the play out and Randy had to run out of bounds  for no gain.  To-Jo and a couple more of us were in hot pursuit awaiting the cutback. To-Jo was yelling, "Stay in bounds Randy, don't run out of bounds."  Center Point tried to break him loose all night, but our defense held firm. Our offensive line was dominating led by Reg and Mauricus. Our backs T. J, Chubb, Mike, and Cam, were running like wild men.  We stopped them on their first drive leading them to punt.  On our first drive, we went right down the field mixing power runs and passes from Wilson.  Mike capped off the first drive on a 20-yard for a score.  Cam scored on the next drive to put us up 12-0, which remained as we went into the second half. The third quarter came, and it's more of the same.  Our defense held them scoreless the entire game.  We poured in two more scores to reach 26 points. I had two interceptions but it should have been three. I caught another one at the end of the game but the official said I trapped it. I'm still  claiming that my hands were under the ball.  So there you have it, the Colts came back to take the championship in dominating fashion 26-0. Center Point played hard but just wasn't good enough that night.  Wow! What an unbelievable season! What a great youth football career! What a way to end it all!  Six years in a row that included undefeated regular seasons. Six years in a row with championship appearances.  Five out of the six years as AYFL Champs.  All of the hard work had paid off.  We went out the same way we started, as Champions. Coach Daryl and all of our coaches were smiling and enjoying every minute of it.  We all hugged and congratulated one another. We also congratulated our opponent for a good game and our former teammate and Colts brother, Randy. As the team walked off the field, guess who was out there waiting with our parents and fans; the cheerleaders and  the famous and dedicated Moms

Squad. You know by now what they were chanting: *"We are proud of you, and we are proud of you."* This time around they had tears in their eyes but not in their hearts. They were tears of joy from a remarkable and incredible six-year run as a team. We met our families, friends, and fans outside the gate. We thanked them for supporting us faithfully over the years. Then we made our way to the locker room still chanting, "We beat them Bulldogs down to the ground, hey hey, we told you yesterday that we were going to clown." In the locker room, we were met by the coaches with our Welch's (champagne) grape juice. Oh what a night! Once everything settled down, all of our coaches spoke and congratulated us on our years of success. Coach Daryl spoke last, and told us he had a Big Announcement. Earlier that week, Coach told us that he received a phone call from the Miracle Strip Bowl in Panama City. They had asked for the winner of our league to come down. They personally asked and hoped it was us. So just when you think it is all over, we had one more item of business left to handle. The team was excited and ready to go back on the road. The news came with positive and negative attributes. The weight class for the tourney was going to be set at 135 lb. That's 15 pounds heavier than where we just finished playing. The positive was that we got to get our quarterback and defensive tackle back in James and Lorenzo came back to play with us as well. The negative was that most of our team was small for a 120 lb weight limit, which would make us even smaller playing at the 135 lb level.

So back at practice, the Colts prepare for our last and final rodeo. All of the guys that had to watched their weight were now free to eat what they wanted. We went back to work challenging each other on every level. We practiced hard; however, we had no film or any idea who our opponents were going to be. All we knew was that there were eight teams invited from the southeast. Just before wrapping up our preparation for the trip, Coach notified us that we were going to be the six seed in the single elimination tournament; a slap in the face to us. The Colts had won 5 of 6 championships with only one loss, and we draw a six seed. We now had some extra motivation to go down there and prove them wrong. We also found out that the team we beat in the finals back on the 85 lb (chapter 3) was the number one seed. Some of the teams were All-Star teams, and we were one of only two teams that actually played at the 120 lb level. The other six teams had already played their season at the 135 lb weight limit. This was supposedly the reasoning for our low seeding. If you ask me, since they requested us, they gave us the hardest road to win it all. In the tourney, we all know that the number one seed plays the number eight and number four plays five. And on the other side; seed number two plays seven and three plays six. So think about it, for us to win it all, we would have to play number three first, possibly number two next, and potentially number one in the finals.

We wrapped up all of our practices and met at the park to load up on the green machine headed back to Florida. Our fans and friends once again followed us. We laughed, joked, and played all the way down there on the bus. Once arriving in Panama, it was crazy. We saw signs up saying: Wanted - Crestwood Colts. I guess the Floridian team Drummond Park wanted revenge from us beating them a couple of years prior. We also heard that they had only lost a hand full of games in six years, one of which was to us. We checked into the hotel and enjoyed the beach all day. Coach met with us later to give the game plan for the next day. On the opening day of games, ironically, we were the first game of the day. We played a team from Tennessee who was the number three seed. These guys were obviously taller and larger than us and were one of the All-Star teams. This Tennessee team was very good and had athletes all over the field. The one thing that they weren't familiar with was our physical style of play. They gave a valiant effort but were not good enough to win. James threw two touchdowns to lead the way to a 28-10 victory. The first game made way for the first upset of the tournament. The six seeded Colts was moving on. After our game, we stayed and watched some of the next game, the two verses seven matchup. The number two seeded team was from Georgia. This team was also huge and loved to throw the ball a bunch. We definitely were going to need to play great pass defense and get pressure on their quarterback to pull the second upset. The coaches and a few Dads stayed and watched all of the games to scout our opponents. The number two team won big over number seven. The number five seed pulled the upset on the four seed on a hail mary pass at the end of the game. And of course, the number one seed destroyed the eighth seed. Now the semifinals are set. Number one will play number five. The Colts were to play number two seed. Of course, our game the next day was set up to be played first. This gave the number one and five seeds a chance to watch us.

Our coaches came back to the room with great information on our opponent. They informed us on all of their shifts and movements. We got up early the next morning and went over some of their formations and tendencies. After that, we left the hotel to head back to the field for our semifinal game against the number two seed from Georgia. Their fans were loud and rowdy similar to ours. The players on their team were tall, huge on the offensive and defensive line, and they had a feisty defense. It took us a little while to get accustomed to their style of play. We fell behind early and was trailing 16-8 at the half. We wasn't playing that bad because this team had been averaging about 50 points per game. We made some adjustments at the half to give them some different looks the second half. We settled down on both sides of the ball to start the third quarter. Midways in the third quarter, we caught a break and ran a fumble in for a score. We converted the two-point conversion to tie the ballgame 16-16. The defense held them scoreless in the second half. Our offense got rolling with two additional scores. We came back to win the ballgame 28-16. After our game, we hung around to watch the next game. Drummond Park demolished the number five seed by a score of 63-8. So the finals were all set up for a rematch (similar to the chapter three on the 85 lb team). Crestwood verses Drummond Park. This time on the 135 lb for all of the marbles. This game could decide who was the best youth football team in the Southeast. And also who was the best Youth football Coach. Just like the Colts, this team, we were told, had only lost a few games in six years, too. They wanted us, and now they got us. After watching the beat down, we left the park to head back to the hotel. Following our physical game, we went out to the beach for some well-needed relaxation. Later that evening, the team watched some film of our opponent from their first two tournament wins. Coach spoke to us afterwards and told us that he would be proud of us no matter what happened the following day. All of the players knew that this time would definitely be our last and final game together. It was exciting and sad at the same time.

The next day rolls around, and we all load up on the bus to head back to the field. Once we arrived, there were Crestwood Wanted signs everywhere. It was like Bon Jovi was singing Dead or Alive upon our entrance. Our fans were confident but yet nervous. This team was going to be our biggest and toughest opponent of the tournament. These guys were huge and very good. All I could think about after seeing this team was the practice game we had against the high school players, the scrimmage on the 100 lb team against our 120 lb. The whole season during the first 120 lb (in chapter six) we were the smaller team in every game. I thought about the scrimmage game against Vestavia as 100 pounders, and they were a 115 lb team. I guess you can say we had our share of experience in these types of games. Coach Daryl led us out with his blue jeans on, cowboy boots, hat, and Crestwood shirt. We're in a single file line and eager to play. The game started and we were having a hard time stopping these guys. We were giving up lots of size at every single position. Their lineman was dominating us up front due to their size. We were going to have to try and use our team speed to win. The problem with this was, they were just as fast as us. We would hold them for the most part near the end zone, but prior to the red zone, they were marching up and down the field on us. Our offensive line was not able to push them back nor open holes for the running backs. Nothing was going right for the Colts. We continued to fight but went into halftime down 14-0. Our coaches made adjustments on offense and defense during the break to help us with their size. The offensive line had to change from one on one blocking to double teaming one person, moving him back and then coming off the block to go and block the linebackers. Defensively we switched from our 5-2 defense to a 4-4 scheme. We placed our defensive lineman in the gaps of their guys. This ultimately freed up our linebackers to make more tackles. We were not winning the one one battles, so we made these adjustments. The second half starts and our changes were starting to work. The offense finally finished a drive and scored a touchdown and two-point conversions to make the score 14-8. We were back in the game, and our fans were elated. The celebration on our end was brief as they ran the ensuing kickoff back to our 2-yard line. They scored and went back up 21-8. So much for the second half momentum. Their score was almost like getting the wind knocked right out you. The fourth quarter came, and we were down 21-8. The guys on the field are yelling 4th quarter our quarter to the sideline while everyone on the sidelines repeated it back. Coach kept telling us to fight to the end. Our first drive in the 4th quarter stalled, and we had to punt the ball away. Finally, we got a break when they mishandled the punt, and we received the ball on their 38-yard-line. Three plays after, we made it to the end zone to make the score 21-14. We missed the extra point to leave the score the same. It was under five minutes left in the game, and they had the ball and the lead. Coach told the defense that we had to get a stop on the upcoming drive. It seemed as if we couldn't stop them as they got first down after first down. They marched down to our 35-yard-line. We stopped them two running plays in a row for no gain. We then had them at a third and ten. They picked up eight yards to leave a fourth and two on our 27-yard-line. They called timeout out and ultimately decided to go for the first down. If they get this first down, we were done. We held our own and stopped the toss sweep short of the first down. This gave our offense one last opportunity to tie the game. With just under two minutes left, we had to go almost 75 yards for a score. James and Wilson execute the two-minute offense to perfection. We mixed some screens, draws and short pass plays to keep them off balance. Ford broke loose on a long run down to their 30-yard-line, before calling timeout. On the next play, we caught a 30-yard touchdown pass with seconds remaining. The score was now 21-20. Coach called a timeout to decide whether to go for one or Go For Two. Everything was on the line, possibly the best youth football team, and maybe the best youth football coach as well. This had to be a tough call for Coach to make; After talking with the assistants, Coach decided to Go For Two. (At this same juncture in chapter three; they overloaded their line to one side and ran a reverse. We stopped them and got the win in the finals.) Coach called a play that overloaded our line to the left. Next we sent our receiver in motion also to the left. All of their coaches were screaming to their players,reverse! reverse! A lot of their players shifted to the strong side. Little did they know that coached called a fake reverse. The toss went right to the weak side, and it looked as if Mike would give the ball to the receiver on the reverse. Instead, he kept the ball and squeezed in for the two-point conversion. We take the lead 22-21. Our crowd and the whole team went crazy. What a comeback! What a play! What a decision to go for the win! We kicked off for one last play as the time expires. We made the tackle to secure the win. Ah man, what a feeling, we were exhausted, yet overwhelmed with joy. We picked Coach up and walked him off the field as a champion. The journey was now complete. Winning the Miracle Strip Tourney was a remarkable way to end six years of greatness. The entire Colts nation was all smiles after this one. We wrapped up the trip and headed back to Birmingham to close the season.

We returned home and later held our final banquet. Coach once again thanked us for allowing him to coach and be our mentor. He had given us so many life lessons that prepared us for our next phase of life. He told us that he would always be there if we needed him. Looking back in life's rear-view mirror, I always wondered what would have happened if we all went to the same high school and played together with Coach. I know that some players weren't going to make it, but to combine those that would have made it with the other local talent would have been great to see. Unfortunately, due to demographics and being from so many different areas and backgrounds, the Colts was separated with players attending different high schools. Some players fell back into the harsh street life that Coach so desperately tried to save them from. Playing for Coach Daryl kept us away from the rugged reality that surrounded us in our rough daily lives. After these six years, it seemed to some as if our protector was gone. Coach later would hire players to work for him back at his machine shop. Coach's prediction made at our last practice before the AYFL championship game was almost exact. We ended up having about 15-20 players to go on and play High School sports. There were approximately seven or eight of us who played sports in college. And finally, there were two players who made it professionally. One was T.J. Slaughter who played with the Jacksonville Jaguars after leaving Southern Miss college and John Carroll High. The next player was Charles (Andy) Rice. He signed with the Pittsburgh Pirates in baseball out of A.H Parker High School in 1993.

To all of my youth league coaches, make sure that you teach the fundamentals of your sport and teach it to every child. I have seen so many instances where coaches only placed the emphasis on the star players instead of the whole team. Every participant deserves your best each day. That's what Coach Daryl showed us every day for six years. You never know which player will make it. We had a ton of talented players just like the two who made it professionally. To parents as well as coaches, your child does not always have to be the quarterback, running back, star basketball, baseball, or soccer player. T.J started at offensive guard on our team on offense and made it to the league. It's not where you play, but it's how you play. It was through hard work, toughness, having a great work ethic, opportunity and perseverance that made the difference.

Finally, our record speaks for itself over a span of six years playing for Coach Daryl. Despite knowing that we played some high school players back in chapter six scrimmage game and lost 6-0, Coach still counted it as a loss. And knowing that (in chapter three) scrimmage game against A. G. where they had the ball 30 minutes and scored eight points, then we got the ball and scored immediately to make it 8-8 as they walked off and quit; Coach Daryl still placed that game as a tie on our plaque. In our eyes after knowing the facts, we didn't count the 6-0 Tarrant scrimmage game as a loss due to them cheating. We saw the A.G. tie game as a win due to them quitting. So whichever one you choose to stand behind, our total record was still a magnificent accomplishment. Coach Daryl's count had us at 87-2-1. The players count was 89-1. Either way, as of this day in September 2017, I still have not seen a team like ours. Therefore I will lay claim that Coach Daryl is the (G.O.A.T.) The Greatest Youth Football Coach of All Time. And with that being said, I will also lay claim that the 1984-1989 Coach Daryl's Crestwood Colts are the Greatest Youth Football Team of All Time.

## Epilogue
### *Going For Two*

In football, there is a tremendous amount of opposition from the defense trying to stop your team from scoring touchdowns and winning. Much like the game of life, there will always be significant opposition to hinder you from reaching your goals and dreams. In the game of football, getting down the field to score can be extremely difficult. In the game of life, we all receive the ball in different areas in which we have no control over. Some people may receive the ball on the fifty-yard line which will make it much easier to score or become successful. We sometimes label these people as being born with a silver spoon in their mouth. Others may receive the ball on the twenty-yard line. These people may have come from a more difficult situation from the beginning of their life. And there are some who may even start on the one-yard line. It seems like life dealt them a lousy hand and success may appear to be so far away or unreachable. When attacking the game of life, remember that the defense has been practicing equally as hard just to stop you. Some people specialize in getting to you, like defensive ends. They work hard every day attempting to get into the backfield and disrupt your goals.

When you have the ball of life, often you will have to depend on others to succeed. You may have coaches and teachers who are mentors to help guide you. There are times where you will have to hand the ball off to your running back to proceed. Meaning that you can't do everything alone. All of us will need help at some point. The most critical support you will need is your offensive line for protection. In the game of life that is God. He will protect and shield you from all hurt, harm, and danger. There will be times that you may fumble the ball, there may be interceptions thrown, and sometimes you may have to punt the ball away. Just like the game of life, you may lose your job; unfair circumstances may cause you to wait your turn for a better position, or push you to reignite your life altogether. Despite all of the situations of life, I believe you can press forward and score your touchdown, if you persevere, keep working hard, and dream big.

In football once you have scored, there is always a decision that has to be made. There has to be an extra point attempt. There are only one of two choices that you can make for an extra point attempt: kick the ball for one point, or run or throw the ball into the end zone for two points. Statistics show that kicking the ball for one has a much higher chance of success than Going For Two. The successful percentage of most teams that choose to go for one is approximately 90-95%. The teams that go for two, the conversion rate is nearly 45%. I believe these numbers are close to being accurate in life as well. I believe 90-95 percent of people will always take the more comfortable and safer route instead of Going For Two. They will only do what's necessary for themselves and not think of others. Going For Two is the more difficult, tougher, and the less popular road traveled.

I am so glad Coach Daryl decided to Go For Two, instead of for one. Our football team almost always went for two on the field; it happened a lot even when we were old enough to kick for one. Going For Two describes Coach Daryl. He always went the extra mile for his team. He instilled in us all of the following: have a strong work ethic, have self-discipline, have fun; stand up to your opposition, believe in yourself, and always push yourself to go the extra mile. He just not only showed us how to be respectable, but he taught us how to handle those who disrespected us. Coach Daryl could have quickly decided to go for one, but instead, he went for two. He would, daily, pick us up for practice and drop us off at home. He helped myself and other players with their annual fee of $50. I can remember times of being sad because I didn't have the money, but coach either paid half of it or all of it for me. It may not seem like much today, but in 1985 man $50 was a lot of money. He went for two by opening up his home to sometimes 30-40 kids. Most of us were African Americans from the projects in Birmingham, AL. Coach Daryl went for two by taking us camping, swimming, out of town, to the beach, prison visits, playing basketball, and baseball. All of this was imperative in keeping us off the streets during the off-season. We learned loads of life lessons on and off the field.

The best way I can describe Coach Daryl is his physical appearance was similar to former Pittsburgh Steelers coach, Bill Cowher, but he coached us like Alabama's current coach, Nick Saban. Can you imagine your 7-year-old playing for Coach Saban? That's the type of discipline we played with every week for six years straight. Since Coach Daryl was an Alabama fan, he would be very proud of the program in 2017. Unfortunately, Coach Daryl lost his battle with cancer back in 2012. (My eyes just filled with water as I wrote that.) I am glad that he had a chance to knock off one of his bucket list items and attend a New York Yankees baseball game before passing (Coach was a huge Yankees fan). Our team, the Colts, could never repay Coach Daryl, in this life or the next. To continue his legacy, I decided that what I can do now is live life as a respectable, dignified man using the same principles he taught us to go and teach others. Presenting yourself as a caring and responsible person who takes care of him or herself is excellent, but it only gives you your touchdown. You still have to decide on your extra point. No matter if you are a parent, foster parent, aunt, uncle, brother, sister, mother figure, father figure, young man, woman or child, you can do something extra to help someone. There is always a person out there that needs your knowledge, love, and support.  My wife and I have fostered over 30 children, so I know first hand about what kids need and the things they are going through. There are kids and youth who need inspiration along with much-needed love. Clothes and shoes are always a necessity. However, kids long for guidance, a listening ear, or being told that they can be somebody. Some of our youth just want to hear that they are unique and loved. I understand that everyone can't be foster parents, but all of us can do something. For example, you can get a child's haircut before going back to school. Or you can purchase a kid a book bag or get a young lady's hair done. The most important thing you can do for a child is to spend time with them. It doesn't necessarily have to be your child. Going to cheer a kid on at one of their sporting or school events, could make their day. You will be surprised at how many kids don't have a cheering section in the crowd. You can Go For Two with adults as well. There are plenty of adults that need jobs, and you may have the influence to push them through; and some seniors need a visit or a helping hand.

Kids, you can also Go For Two. If your parents are fortunate enough to buy you some J's or shoes costing $200; then you are blessed. However they may be a kid in your class who needs some shoes but their parents may not be able to afford them. The next time your parents give you the opportunity to purchase a $200 pair of shoes, tell them that you would like to share by offering a kid in need an $75 pair shoes, while you take an $75 pair and this act of kindness saves your parents $50.  Doing what I have mentioned here, makes a huge difference in someone's life.

In my final thoughts, I request that you ask yourself the following questions:

1: Have you scored your touchdown? ( Being a responsible, loving, respectable, caring person and friend who takes care of yourself.)

2: Are you Going For One? (Taking care of yourself, your immediate responsibilities such as your kids and family. )

3: Are you Going For Two? (Taking care of yourself, your responsibilities and helping someone that's in need that's not your immediate responsibility.)

If we all take Coach Daryl's mentality to not only score, not only go for one, but to Go For Two to help someone else, I believe in my heart that our relationships, our communities, and this world would be a better and safer place for us all.

I've made up my mind up a long time ago
I'm gonna Go For Two

The question I ask you is
What are you going to do?

Join the movement to change the world at www.gofor2.net

54262996R00102

Made in the USA
Columbia, SC
29 March 2019